W9-CSS-425

SAKE
CONFIDENTIAL

a beyond-the-basics guide to
UNDERSTANDING, TASTING, SELECTION & ENJOYMENT

John Gauntner

Stone Bridge Press • Berkeley, California

*To Providence, for its support,
and to Mayu, for hers*

Published by
Stone Bridge Press
P. O. Box 8208, Berkeley, CA 94707
sbp@stonebridge.com • www.stonebridge.com

Enjoy sake sensibly and responsibly!

Text © 2014 John Gauntner.

Book design and layout by Linda Ronan.

Printed in the United States of America.

10 9 8 7 6 5 4 3 2 1   2018 2017 2016 2015 2014

This book is available in both print and digital editions:
p-ISBN: 978-1-61172-014-3
e-ISBN: 978-1-61172-551-3

CONTENTS

FOREWORD

One of the most appealing aspects of sake, in my opinion, is that it is both simple and complex at the same time. And this same observation can be applied to just about any aspect of the sake world.

For starters, one needs to know very little about sake to begin to appreciate it. It's usually fairly priced, so the more you pay, the more you get. Drink *ginjo* to stay safely in the top 10 percent. Drink it young and slightly chilled. Using wine glasses works well. That right there is enough to carry you far and allow you to enjoy sake without further knowledge.

However, there are exceptions to each one of those seemingly simple principles, and that is where sake really gets interesting. Go just below the surface of the basics, and an incredibly broad, subtle, and deliciously vague world opens up to you.

Remember, it is okay to keep things simple! But if you choose to embark upon it, the sake path is long, winding, and immensely interesting.

This applies to sake flavors and aromas, production, culture, and more. I find this to be the case with many things in Japan, including sumo, cuisine, and especially the language. Without any effort on my part, this book has ended up that way, too, almost as if the sake itself imparted its essence on the flow of the text.

Reading the Introduction alone will very quickly make the sake world approachable and accessible, allowing you to get out there and enjoy it now. But as you read on, you will

encounter in each chapter and section an introduction to concepts that build on the first bits,
then open doors that lead to whole vistas of
information. Much of this information is con-
tradictory and vague, all of which makes sake so
fascinating.

The conflicting aspects of sake may have
served different purposes at different times,
but today, such conflicts lead to many misperceptions. As we try to unwind these misperceptions, sake only becomes more interesting.
Consider temperature, for example. Sake is well
known as one of the few alcoholic beverages
that can be enjoyed warm. Yet we hear that premium sake is usually best served chilled. So why
does hot sake seem to be the go-to choice at
so many venues? We may hear, too. of a trend
in gently warming premium sake, or conversely,
of the silly idea that sake is warmed to hide the
flaws. What is the truth?

In the handful of conflicting truths peace-
fully coexisting is the true appeal of sake.

Beyond this are many other facets of sake,
such as aging, vessels, pasteurization, and perceived purity—topics on which people take
sides, sometimes with strong opinions. Profound differences of opinion can also be found
concerning the impossibly detailed sake-making process, how sake is enjoyed, the structure
of the industry, and the philosophies of the
major players in the industry.

While simply drinking sake may be plea-
surable enough, getting under the hood and
learning more about sake—including some of
the more controversial and otherwise fascinating aspects of the sake world—makes the experience even more enjoyable.

ACKNOWLEDGMENTS

As I look back over the past two decades of involvement with the sake world, one thing is glaringly obvious: I did not choose this sake path; it chose me. In fact, I do not even recall having ever made the concrete decision to make sake my job. I arrived in Japan in 1988 on a "one year" teaching program. A respected coworker introduced me to half a dozen good sake on New Year's Day 1989, and from that point I was fascinated, and in love. But I never thought I would ever make sake my work. One chance meeting after another, one coincidence after another, led to a newspaper column, which led to a book, which led to the need to learn more, which led to involvement with the industry. And the circle continues.

Deciding where to begin expressing my gratitude is daunting. It is, after all, a circle. Let it start with Masao Anzai, who introduced me to the stuff. And let it continue with Rick Warm, Bryan Harrell, David Friedman, Mark Thompson, David Dow, Grif Frost, and Yishane Lee, who all played their part in getting me started in properly writing articles, books, websites, and the like.

Once I became involved in the sake industry, the list of those that helped further the cause just expanded exponentially. In particular, Yasutaka Daimon of Daimon Brewery, Yuichiro Tanaka and his late father Takejiro of Rihaku Brewery, and Kosuke Kuji of Nanbu Bijin Brewery immediately come to mind as three sake brewers who have encouraged, supported, and helped me in ways more than I can ever hope to repay. Every single one of the hundreds of *sakagura* I have visited over the last twenty years has truly inspired me, generously shared with me incredible information, and conveyed their passion for their craft and their product. Not one iota of it has been lost on me. There are, doubtlessly, countless others who have also been a part of this path.

Thanks as well to my friend Haruo Matsuzaki, who has taught me more about sake than anyone on the planet. And of course, very sincere gratitude goes to Philip Harper of Tamagawa Shuzo, who has taught me tons and exposed me to so much of the world of sake, both directly and indirectly. There is also Hitoshi Utsunomiya and everyone at the National Research Institute of Brewing to be thanked for technical information and skills I somehow managed to pick up along the way.

Next, appreciation goes out to Ed Lehrman, Nick Ramkowsky, and everyone else at Vine Connections, who provided me with opportunities to leave the confines of my sake-appreciation bubble and learn market realities, which has been invaluable. Mark Schumacher has helped me immensely with so much, including but not limited to getting the good word out in a good format to the thirsty masses in the U.S. Thanks as well to the more than one thousand people who have taken my professional course, as nothing makes us learn a subject more than teaching it.

Inanimate though it *might* be, thanks to sake itself for being so damn interesting and so damn tasty, and to Matsuo-sama, the Shinto god of sake, for watching over us all for so long.

And finally but most importantly to my wife, Mayuko, who has not only tolerated but has actually enthusiastically supported this silliness for so long.

John Gauntner
Kamakura, Japan

INTRODUCTION

This book comprises over two dozen chapters that go into a fair amount of depth about all things sake. Just about every topic is covered, revealing pros and cons, honest realities, and behind-the-scenes candor.

Perhaps, then, it is best to quickly cover some basic ground about sake in this introduction, which will make it easier to go through the rest of the chapters in any order you choose. So, here, let us run through the basics of sake, what it is and how it is made, and what terms and concepts you really need to know to enjoy it right away. Most of the topics covered lightly here are presented in much more detail in the main chapters.

What Is Sake?

In short, sake is an alcoholic beverage that is brewed from rice. While this may seem obvious, there are two important points revealed here.

One, in terms of fermentable materials, sake is made from rice only. No other grains or sugars are fermented in the sake-making process. While water, yeast, and a mold known as *koji* are used, no other fermentable materials are used.

Two, sake is a brewed beverage. It is not a simple fermentation like wine, nor is it a distilled beverage like whiskey. It is closer to a beer than anything else but is nonetheless unique.

Sake's alcohol content is about 15–16 percent, which is only a bit higher than a robust red wine. This is watered down from the naturally occurring 20 percent or so simply for enjoyability, since the higher alcohol content overpowers subtle aromas and flavors.

Sake production is unique in many ways. Beer is made by converting starches in barley to sugar using enzymes that arise when the barley is malted—that is, when it is moistened, warmed, and allowed to sprout. Sake, however, is made from white rice, which is rice that has had the brown outer part—the husk—milled away. This means that it cannot be malted the way barley is for making beer, but enzymes are still needed to chop the long starch molecules into smaller, bite-size sugar molecules. These sugar molecules can be gobbled up by the yeast cells, which then give off alcohol and carbon dioxide.

In sake brewing, these enzymes are provided courtesy of *koji* mold (its scientific name is *Aspergillus oryzae*). The spores of this mold are sprinkled on about 20–25 percent of all the rice that goes into a batch of sake, and as this mold grows around and into the grains of steamed rice, it gives off the necessary enzymes, which then convert the starch in the rice into sugar.

In beer, the starch-to-sugar conversion and sugar-to-alcohol fermentation take place separately and sequentially. However, in sake brewing, the moldy rice trickles sugar into the mash in the same space and at the same time that the yeast cells convert said sugar into alcohol.

The process is referred to as "multiple parallel fermentation" and represents a difficult balance to strike. It yields the highest naturally occurring alcohol level of any non-distilled beverage on the planet: the aforementioned 20 percent.

The History and Process of Making Sake

How long has sake been around? The short answer is about a thousand years. It has been about that long since sake came to resemble what we enjoy today, in both production methods and in the nature of the completed product.

But in reality, sake has been around for about 1,700 years. Back then, someone left some steamed rice lying around, upon which naturally occurring *koji* mold and yeast fell. That led to an oatmeal-like, mash-like sake.

Premium *ginjo* sake, however, with all its refined complexity and aromatic style, has only been on the market as a viable product for about forty years. This is not to imply sake was a lesser beverage before *ginjo*; not at all. It was just as good, if less ostentatious.

To make sake, rice harvested in the fall is milled, then soaked and steamed. *Koji* mold is grown on about a quarter of it. Next, a yeast starter (*moto*) is created in a small vat from a mixture of the *koji* rice, regular steamed rice, water, and yeast. Here a very high concentration of yeast cells develops. This is to ensure that when wild yeast or bacteria drop into the tank, the correct yeast will be so abundant that there will be no adverse effects.

To this small yeast starter, more *koji* rice, steamed rice, and water are added at three different times over four days to keep the yeast population from thinning out too much. This mixture—the mash or *moromi*—is allowed to ferment for about twenty to forty days, then the rice lees that did not completely liquefy are filtered away. After that, the just-completed sake will be pasteurized, filtered, and stored, traditionally for six months. Then it is diluted a bit, pasteurized again, and bottled.

This is the gist of the process. From start to finish, it takes six to eight weeks for production, then about six months for maturation. But there are countless variations and exceptions.

Good Sake and Less-Good Sake

Let's face it: there is almost no bad sake out there anymore. Nothing properly cared for will make you cringe. There are, of course, factors that make one sake good but another great.

However, before we get to that, here is a concept that makes sake extremely approachable. While not everyone will completely agree with this, I stand by it: 90 percent of the time, sake is fairly priced, and you will get what you pay for. Naturally, if your preferences in sake are clear—if you know what you like—then defer to those rather than price in making a decision. But should you not know what you like, or anything about the selections before you, making a decision based on price will work 90 percent of the time.

Are there are exceptions? Of course. There are exceptions to everything in the sake world. There are sake that are overpriced and sake that are deals. But these will make up perhaps one bottle out of ten, so 90 percent of the time you can make a decision based on price, feel safe about it, then relax and enjoy the sake you have chosen.

Furthermore, if you always drink sake with the word *ginjo* somewhere on the bottle, you will always enjoy sake that is ensconced in the realm of the super premium.

Next, since sake is fairly priced 90 percent of the time, let's consider what affects price and quality—what it is that makes one sake relatively inexpensive and mundane, while another is quite pricey and tastes and smells like ambrosia from heaven?

In short, there are three things that affect price and quality: rice, milling, and craftsmanship.

Rice

Just as good wine is made from grapes that are quite different from those we buy at the grocery store, good sake is made from rice that is significantly different from rice that we eat. Note that not all sake is made from proper sake rice; however, almost all premium sake is.

There are a handful of differences between sake rice and regular rice. Sake rice plants are taller, and the grains are about 30 percent larger and with more starch and less fat and protein than regular rice. Furthermore, the starch that will be converted into sugar, and subsequently into alcohol, is physically concentrated in the center of each grain. Surrounding that, near the surface of the rice grain, are fat and protein.

In regular rice, these are more mixed up within the grain, and the color is pretty much uniform throughout because the fats, proteins, and starches are more evenly distributed. But in sake rice, we can see a white center in many of the grains where the starch is concentrated. The fat and protein are located in the surrounding, more translucent region closer to the surface of the grain. This is significant because rice constructed this way can be milled more effectively so as to remove the fat and protein hovering near the surface, leaving only the desirable starch behind.

These differences in content make table rice taste better than sake rice. While you can eat sake rice if you want to, it is about three times as expensive as table rice, and it does not taste as good.

Just like grapes for wine, there are many different varieties of sake rice, all with their own character and levels of quality, and these lead to different flavors and aromas in the final sake. Again like grapes, different varieties of sake rice have regions and climates in which they thrive. However, sake rice can legally and easily be shipped around Japan for use by brewers (*toji*) in regions other than where it was grown.

Milling

The second thing that makes one sake better and more expensive than another is how much the rice has been milled. Why is this important?

As explained above, in proper sake rice,

the starches that will ferment are physically located in the center of the grain. Around that, near the outer portion of the grain, are fats and proteins. This means that the more we mill the rice, the more we remove the less desirable fat and protein, and the more easily we can access the sought-after starch. In fact, a great generalization—with plenty of exceptions—is that the more you mill the rice before brewing, the better the sake will be. Of course, more milling drives costs up, since you need more rice to get the same job done, but it is worth it in the end.

The amount that the rice has been milled is referred to as the *seimai-buai* (pronounced "say my booh eye") and is expressed as a percentage of the grain's original size that remains after milling. If the *seimai-buai* is listed as 60 percent, that means the rice was milled before brewing so that only 60 percent of the original size of the grains remained (i.e., the outer 40 percent was ground away and was not used in the brewing process).

Craftsmanship

The third thing that makes one sake better and more expensive than another is the labor-intensive, hand-crafted effort that has gone into making it. In other words, sake can be made by machine or by hand. Perhaps 80 percent of sake is made using automated processes, and much of this sake is just fine and can be very enjoyable. However, almost without exception, the best sake is made by hand.

Each step of the sake-making process becomes the foundation for the next, and the success of any step depends hugely on all that has come before it. So, quality resulting from painstaking effort early on is carried through to the end. How the rice is washed, soaked, and steamed affects the *koji* making, which in turn affects the fermentation, and this chain continues until the product is complete.

★ ★ ★

In review, then, the three things that make one sake better and more expensive than another are:

1. Rice: Good sake rice is expensive, but worth it.
2. Milling: Generally, the more the rice is milled, the higher the quality of sake.
3. Labor: More often than not, hand-crafted, labor-intensive techniques lead to better sake.

The Grades of Sake

The illustration on the next page shows the grades of sake at a glance, and their legal definitions. The higher up the "river" you go, the higher the grade of sake, the more expensive the sake, and the more highly milled the rice must be to qualify for that grade.

All the grades of premium sake (*junmai-shu* and *honjozo*, *junmai ginjo* and *ginjo*, and *junmai daiginjo* and *daiginjo*) are *legally* defined by little more than how much the rice was milled before brewing. That's how important milling is.

To make learning about sake as easy as possible, consider this point: if you remember just one word about the grades of sake, let it be *ginjo*. *Ginjo* sake is to regular sake what single malt scotch is to regular scotch, or what 100 percent agave tequila is to regular tequila. It is the same stuff, but made with better raw materials and using more exacting methods to arrive at a better product. If you always drink sake with the word *ginjo* somewhere on the bottle, you will always be in the safe zone.

However, be aware that there is a lot of overlap between the premium grades of sake, and that almost no one can always tell what class a sake belongs to just by tasting it.

So learn the grades, but do not get hung up on them.

The top four grades of sake as a group are referred to as *ginjo-shu* and along with regular *junmai* and *honjozo* make up the six premium sake grades collectively known as *tokutei meishoshu* or "special designation sake."

Namazake, nigorizake, genshu, koshu, and other sake types are available in every grade.

Junmai-shu

Tokubetsu Junmai-shu

JUNMAI SAKE
Brewed with rice, water, and *koji* (no alcohol added)

Seimai-buai (% rice remaining after milling)

70% or less*

60% or less

Honjozo-shu

Tokubetsu honjozo-shu

NON-JUNMAI SAKE
Brewed with rice, water, *koji*, and a small amount of distilled alcohol

Premium sake

Normal "table" sake

"REGULAR" SAKE
No minimum milling requirement and with larger amounts of alcohol added (65% of the market)

* *Seimai-buai* for *junmai* sake can exceed 70% but *honjozo* must be 70% or less.

Junmai daiginjo-shu

Junmai ginjo-shu

50% or less

Daiginjo-shu

Ginjo-shu

Increasing quality, price, fragrance, complexity

SAKE GRADES AT A GLANCE

Futsu-shu

You may have noticed that *ginjo* has four subclasses: *junmai ginjo* (which has no added alcohol); regular *ginjo* (which has some added alcohol); *junmai daiginjo* (no added alcohol); and regular *daiginjo* (some added alcohol). All four are collectively known as *ginjo*.

Junmai *Types and Non-*junmai *Types*

Note that the largest pool in our sake river is labeled *futsu-shu*, or regular (table) sake. This is non-premium sake, and it represents the lion's share of the market. Sake in this realm has been cut with relatively large amounts of pure distilled alcohol for economic reasons. Note that a lot of this sake is truly very enjoyable, but it is not premium sake.

The several grades of premium sake shown at the top of the river are collectively known as *tokutei meishoshu*, or "special designation sake."

Among these, anything with the word *junmai* in it is made using only rice, water, and *koji* (the enzyme-rich moldy rice), with no added alcohol.

However, the three sake types within this premium realm that do not include the word *junmai*—i.e., *honjozo*, *ginjo*, and *daiginjo*—are made by adding some distilled alcohol at the end of the brewing process.

In these types, the alcohol is added for very good technical reasons and not to increase yields as it is in *futsu-shu* regular sake. These reasons include, most significantly, helping to extract aromas and flavors from the fermenting mash. Many of the compounds in the mash are soluble in alcohol; adding a bit of distilled alcohol just after fermentation is complete raises the overall alcohol content, which allows more flavor and aroma to be pulled out. Note that water is later added to bring the alcohol back down to the usual 16 percent so that such sake is not fortified. It just had a higher alcohol level at one stage of its development. Adding alcohol has other benefits too, including smoothening the product and improving stability and shelf life.

There are purists who insist only the *junmai* types are valid sake, but in truth, neither type (*junmai* or non-*junmai*) is unequivocally better than the other.

Other Types of Sake

Here are a few more types of sake that you may see indicated on a label. These terms have no legal relationship to grade, meaning that these sake types can come in all grades.

Nigorizake is cloudy sake, sake in which some of the lees have been purposely left behind. Creamier, chewier, and richer, it is a throwback to sake of centuries past, and to moonshine as well.

Namazake is sake that has not been pasteurized. It can be fresh, zippy, and lively, but it is not necessarily better than pasteurized sake.

Genshu is undiluted sake, usually but not always of a higher alcohol content, perhaps 19–20 percent.

Yamahai and *kimoto* are styles made with a yeast starter prepared in a way that usually leads to a gamier, richer, earthier flavor profile.

Koshu and *choki-jukuseishu* both refer to aged sake.

Kijoshu is sake made using already completed sake in place of some water. It is a sweet, rich dessert sake. Very little is produced.

What of **sparkling sake**? There is some out there, but it is relatively new on the market, and a comparatively minuscule number of carbonated products exist. While it can be enjoyable, it is quite a different animal from regular sake.

The Nihonshu-do

Sometimes called the "Sake Meter Value" in English, the *nihonshu-do* refers to the specific gravity of the sake, i.e., the density of the sake compared to the density of water. More practically, it is a number typically between -3 and +12 that indicates the sweetness or dryness of a sake. It is entirely unrelated to grade and quality.

Theoretically, the higher (more positive) the number, the drier the sake. The lower (more negative) the number, the sweeter the sake. Just remember, "Higher is dryer." Note that zero is not neutral in terms of sweet or dry, but rather indicates the exact same density as pure water. The average *nihonshu-do* these days is about +4 or so.

However, this number is not all that useful except in its extreme manifestations, since so many things affect the perception of sweet and dry.

Aging Sake

Almost all sake is not aged but is consumed young. One should not collect or store sake, but rather drink it soon after purchase. Sake will begin to noticeably change in flavor and aroma after about a year.

Some sake is aged, however, and can be interesting. But unlike wine, what little sake is aged is aged in varying ways with varying results. Aged sake is definitely not better than its youthful counterpart. Sake usually benefits from a few months of maturation, but it is almost always meant to be consumed young and fresh. Just remember that there are a few tasty exceptions.

Temperature

Most premium sake like *ginjo* should be consumed slightly chilled. There are of course the requisite exceptions. In fact, there is a bit of a warmed-sake renaissance going on in Japan now. So enjoy your sake—and your *ginjo* in particular—slightly chilled (about white wine temperature), but know that some are very enjoyable gently warmed.

Vessels and Glassware for Enjoying Sake

Wine glasses work fine, especially for aromatic *ginjo*, although stemware is rarely used in Japan. However, even if it does not flatter flavors and enhance aromas as well, traditional Japanese pottery adds a very enjoyable tactile and visual appeal to sake drinking. And, most importantly, there is no one perfect shape of glass, no matter what anyone tells you.

Storage

Storing sake is simple: treat it like a wine. In other words, keep it cool and out of strong light. It does not need to be refrigerated unless it is *namazake* (unpasteurized sake). Since colder temperatures will slow down aging and not hurt the sake at all, if you have room in the refrigerator, keep it there!

Once a bottle is open, the safest thing is to treat it like a bottle of wine and drink it soon (which is not usually a problem). Some sake lasts longer than others, and generally sake is more forgiving than wine. As a rule of thumb, after opening you have about a week.

Sake and Food

Sake and food pairing follows the same principles as wine and food pairings: look for things that complement and enhance aspects of both the food and the sake. There are no rules! By no means should sake be limited to Japanese food, or even to Asian food. While mismatches are certainly possible, there is a very wide range of Western food with which sake dovetails wonderfully.

Surely, very strongly flavored and spicy dishes are mismatches, as the subtle aspects of sake will be drowned out. After removing obviously incongruous pairings from the equation experiment with all forms of fish, vegetables, and even lightly prepared meats. You will be pleasantly surprised at how versatile sake can be.

★ ★ ★

The above is a quick rundown of all the pillars of knowledge you need to enjoy sake simply and soon. Each one of these points presented can be expanded upon greatly. That is what the rest of this book does—going into almost excruciating detail and mild controversy about each of the important topics pertaining to sake.

Using This Book

This book is designed as a basic reference to which you can return again and again. You can read the chapters in order, but you don't have to. At the back I've provided a glossary and an index to help you find what you're looking for and learn the sake vocabulary you come across as you read.

Within each chapter is a sidebar featuring a particular sake that pertains to the subject under discussion. I've tried to pick sake that are available outside Japan, but importers are constantly changing their selections, so you may not always be able to find a particular bottle.

I want to be open and state up front that I do have a business interest in the importation to the U.S. of four of the sake introduced in this book. They were ideal for the topics in their respective chapters, so I thought it best to introduce them. Those four sake are Amanoto, Fukucho, Tensei, and Yuho.

J.G.

SAKE SECRETS

Junmai vs. Non-Junmai

How *junmai* grades compare to non-*junmai* grades—how sake made with only rice, water, and *koji* compares to sake made with these three ingredients plus a bit of pure distilled alcohol—is a topic of interest in the sake world. Opinions are varied, to say the least.

In some circles there almost seems to be a vendetta against anything that is not of the *junmai* style. There are a handful of reasons why this is so, although none seems totally valid, and a couple are not even correct. Some folks insist the rice-only *junmai* method is the only true, real way to make sake, or that to add alcohol is almost cheating. Others insist they cannot stand the taste of the added alcohol, or that it gives them a hangover. Such detractors do not even consider acknowledging the ways in which non-*junmai* sake can actually be better than *junmai*!

When we look at all sake produced today, just over 65 percent is *futsu-shu*, or regular "table sake." During the production of this lowest grade of sake, good dollops of alcohol are indeed added, and for purely economic reasons. By adding alcohol brewers can significantly improve if not stretch yields, and for many consumers on the street, sake like that is good enough. And in truth, most of that grade of sake is perfectly enjoyable. Certainly not *premium,* but enjoyable nonetheless.

Moving into the realm of premium sake— the top 35 percent—anything that does not have the word *junmai* as a prefix is also made with a bit of added alcohol. While there are limits to how much can be added even to *futsu-shu*, it is limited further in the premium sake classes.

But here is what is really significant: when alcohol is added during production to what will become premium sake, it is not done for economic reasons. It is done for sound, technical reasons.

Like what? you might ask.

Well, for starters, aroma and flavor. Some flavor and aroma compounds are soluble in alcohol. If a bit of alcohol is added to the fermenting mash just after fermentation is complete but before the sake is separated from the lees, it becomes easier to draw those flavors and aromas out of the rice and get them into the sake. The temporary increase of alcohol just before pressing helps sake become more aromatic at the least. It also adds to shelf life and stability.

Amanoto "Heaven's Door" Tokubetsu Junmai
ASAMAI SHUZO KK, AKITA

Butter-n-raisin flavors and smoky, earthy, sweet aromas.

Few *kura* are as particular about the locality of their rice as this one. Proximity is paramount. Not only must it all be local Akita rice, but as much as possible it should come from rice fields visible from the roof of the *kura*. So it seemed only natural when they made their output a hundred percent *junmai* types; no added-alcohol sake at all. Nevertheless, they still maintain creativity and variety across their products.

There is a word in Japanese, *aru-ten,* which is an abbreviation for *arukoru tenka,* or "added alcohol." It is an industry term, not an official one, and it is not found on labels. But it is a less unwieldy way to refer to all non-*junmai* sake collectively, so let us use it here.

Statistics clearly show that consumption of *junmai* types collectively (i.e., *junmai-shu, junmai ginjo,* and *junmai daiginjo*) is growing, albeit minutely. *Junmai* fans love to point this out. But what is really happening is that both *futsu-shu* and *honjozo* consumption are dropping—not because they are *aru-ten,* but rather because fewer people are drinking lower grades of sake. The bottom of the market is contracting, but the bottom is so large (and consists of all *aru-ten!*) that it skews perception.

In truth, a closer look at statistics will show that production of all the top grades, including the *aru-ten* versions of *ginjo* and *daiginjo,* is growing slowly but surely. The point is that *aru-ten* is not contracting in the face of preferences for *junmai,* but rather that premium sake is being chosen over cheap sake.

Another myth about *junmai* is that it was the original and proper method of making sake, and that adding alcohol only came about in the 1940s due to wartime rice shortages and other related reasons. In fact, as far back as several centuries some brewers would from time to time add distilled alcohol to bolster a weakly fermenting tank of sake. So the technique is neither new nor non-traditional. It is very much a part of the incredible skill and masterful techniques of the craft of brewing sake in Japan.

Originally, all *ginjo* sake was *aru-ten.* When *ginjo* brewing methods were being developed, adding alcohol at the end was an integral step. If one was going to go to that extent to bring out flavor and aroma, that step was considered indispensable. The *junmai* versions of *ginjo* and *daiginjo* came later in the 20th century.

Then there are those who insist they can smell and taste the difference. Admittedly, in cheap sake this is easy, as the overall component balance is thin, lacking umami, or is unbalanced in sweetness. But in the realm of the *ginjo* levels, this is not a valid argument. The final alcohol content is the same as non–*aru-ten*, what was added was strictly limited, and it is all the same thing: ethyl alcohol.

An even greater misconception is that *aru-ten* sake is fortified. Sure, for a short period of time it was fortified, but it was watered back down to the same 16 percent or so before being shipped. Certainly this point is debatable, but it seems to me that if it is not fortified when we enjoy it, it is not a fortified drink.

A very rough estimation shows that on average, *aru-ten* is about 15 percent cheaper than a corresponding *junmai*. In other words, if two sake are made from the same rice milled to the same degree, the *aru-ten* will be about 15 percent cheaper, but often, thanks to the *aru-ten* process, it will be just as lively and enjoyable. Certainly this point, too, is debatable, but that is how it seems to me. So *aru-ten* wins the cost-performance competition as well.

Finally, 90 percent of the sake market in Japan is *aru-ten* sake. And a lot of it is truly outstanding sake! It seems inappropriate to summarily "diss" most of what is out there, since it is obviously valid if it makes up most of the market.

Looking at the whole question from a different angle, since the mid-1990s many brewers seem to be maximizing the potential of the two styles. In other words, *junmai* types have the potential to be richer, a bit higher in acidity, and fuller. More and more *junmai* sake are heading in that direction, particularly in comparison to their *aru-ten* counterparts, which tend to be more aromatic and lighter. Sure, there are tons of exceptions either way, but it seems that more brewers try to make *junmai* types more *junmai*-

esque, so to speak, and to maximize what adding alcohol can do.

Currently, there are twenty-five to thirty *kura* that make only *junmai*. (A sake brewer in Japan is called a *sakagura*, often shortened to just *kura*.) While this number is increasing, it is still a drop in the bucket of the 1,200 that currently exist. That is not quite enough to call it a trend.

In the end, being a *junmai* purist is fine. People are free to be purists; it is certainly the right of any consumer. There is joy in that. But know that should you go that route, you are cutting yourself off from a *lot* of good stuff.

I am personally not anti-*junmai*. In fact, I surely drink more *junmai* types than *aru-ten* types. I am, instead, for avoiding hype from misinformation. As good as *junmai*, *junmai ginjo*, and *junmai daiginjo* are, they are not *unequivocally* better than their *aru-ten* counterparts.

Namazake

Namazake, i.e., sake that has not been pasteurized, is another topic that could benefit from some clarification. *Nama* can sometimes be more youthful, fresh, zippy, and lively than sake that has been pasteurized. It is of course much less stable and must be kept quite cold to ensure it does not go bad. However, *namazake* (the *s* of "sake" becomes a *z* in this compound) as a category is *not* indisputably better than its pasteurized counterpart.

Almost all sake on the market has been pasteurized by heating it. This is done to stabilize sake, as there are bacteria in the air that can, if present, feed on by-products of enzymatic activity remaining from the *koji*. Heat deactivates the *koji* and exterminates the bacteria. Since cold temperatures restrain that detrimental activity, a sake that has not been pasteurized will be spared undue damage if kept refrigerated.

In the past, *namazake* was rare, in part because producers could not guarantee that everyone to whom their sake was distributed would handle it properly. Long ago, one could only drink *namazake* at the *kura*. Even today, it is a very small part of the overall sake market. Perhaps that gives it a sense of being rare and special, which many people find appealing. However, pasteurized sake is not a lesser manifestation. It's just different; that's all. In fact, the two types are very different. If, for example, half of a given batch of sake were to be pasteurized and the other half left as *nama*, how the two would taste and smell immediately afterward and the paths of maturation they would take would be forever altered—and never the twain shall meet. But neither one would be better than the other.

It is true that *nama* has an immediate appeal. The fresh, lively aromatics often (but not always!) found in *nama* can draw one in and evoke an immediate, positive response. However, that same ostentatious aspect is something common to almost all *nama* and can actually get in the way of subtler, deeper aspects of the sake. To me, very often the *nama*-esque qualities of a sake create a veil that prevents me from seeing into its depths.

In other words, I smell and taste a sake and think, "It's *nama*." While that alone is not at all unappealing, that's it; I'm done. I know right there that I am not being shown the entire picture, that I would be able to sense more about the sake if it had been pasteurized. This does not mean I can tell nothing else about a sake— there are still countless things to enjoy: aromatic compounds, flavors, textures, volume, acidity. . . . However, at the same time I realize subtlety and depth are among those aspects to which I will not be treated if the sake is *nama*. And that, often, is disappointing.

To avoid exaggeration, let me point out that not all *namazake* present the obscuring veil. There are certainly *namazake* that exhibit nuanced depth and enjoyable complexity. The issue is that such qualities are very hard to maintain against the enemies of time, temperature, and oxygen. As good as such sake may be, it is not overtly superior; it is just good for what it is. To me, with *namazake* there is little to be gained and much at risk.

Why do I belabor this point? Because all too often I see everyone in the distribution chain— from producers to distributor sales staff and even restaurants and retailers—touting *nama* as special or hailing it as better. Surely, while marketing their products is important (and we consumers love the special and rare), this kind of misinformation can adversely affect long-term understanding and appreciation of sake.

Of course, opinions vary, and there are different ideas about what is important to maintain in a sake. If, for example, you prefer sake that is as close as possible to what it was when it was brewed, by all means *nama* will approach that ideal. There are inherent risks, as there are with any predilection, but it is nonetheless a valid way to assess sake.

A few more technical points about pasteurization or the lack thereof will be useful. Most sake is actually pasteurized twice: once after brewing is completed, and a second time when it moves from storage tanks to bottles. Any time the sake is exposed to the air there is a chance that offending bacteria might sneak their way in. Heating it will minimize the chances of damage.

However, if care is taken, one of the two

Kazenomori Junmai Ginjo

YUCHO SHUZO KK, NARA

Apple and pear aromas imbued with freshness. Creamy, full, and rich flavor with a sharp, banana-tinged finish.

The brewery makes another brand as well, but the Kazenomori brand is all *namazake*. In an effort to impart the quality of their water and their rice as well as the skill of their *toji*, as little as possible is done to the sake between tank and bottle. As such, this sake is also all *junmai*, all *muroka*, and all *genshu*. It is pressed in a unique way that keeps oxygen out and freshness in.

can be skipped without sacrificing stability. If a sake is pasteurized once before storage and protected from the ambient air on its way to the bottle, the second of the two pasteurizations is not necessary. Alternatively, if it is kept cold enough on the way to and during maturation storage but is properly pasteurized on the way to the bottle, the first of the two can be eliminated.

When the first pasteurization is skipped, the product is called *nama-chozo* (stored *nama*), and if the second one is omitted it is called *nama-tsume* (bottled *nama*). A seasonal variation on the latter seen only in the fall is *hiya-oroshi*, but technically it is the same.

While these variants may seem gimmicky, the goal is to maintain some sense of the sake's youth but also provide stability. My diatribe notwithstanding, the less pasteurization the better. In the old days, which ended perhaps in the 1980s, the priority was to ensure the sake did not go bad, as that would be literally revenue down the drain. Back then, pasteurization was a much more punishing process. But as technical understanding has progressed, brewers have learned to pasteurize using a myriad of new ways, like lightning-quick heat exchangers, or hot-then-cold showers over just-filled bottles. There are countless opinions about which methods are best, but techniques are much more advanced and supportive of the sake these days.

Instead of the term *namazake* to refer to unpasteurized sake, the term *nama-nama* or *hon-nama* is sometimes used to emphasize that the sake was not pasteurized even once, that the brewer didn't even *think* about pasteurizing it. But these three terms—*namazake, nama-nama,* and *hon-nama*—all mean the same thing.

Another factoid worth remembering is that just because a sake is *nama* does not guarantee it will go bad if not refrigerated. If the *kura* in which it was produced is clean enough, there is a good chance that bacteria never entered the sake in the first place. But the potential for *namazake* to go south is significantly higher if it is not kept refrigerated

Just how cold is cold enough? There is no one absolute temperature that is best, but in general, colder is better. Arguably, 5°C (41°F) is safe, and a few degrees higher would not be disastrous. "Cold enough" is a matter of one's threshold for trouble. An hour or two out of the refrigerator will not affect anything, nor will the time spent on a plane ride home from Japan. Nor will a day, or even two. But after that, it is time to heed the principles involved and time to get it back to a cold environment.

Namazake can "go bad" if not kept cold, but just how bad is bad is not a black-and-white issue. At first, especially if oxygen is involved, *namazake* will head south by exhibiting more of what makes it enjoyable: prominent aromas that, while not unpleasant, can be woody and cloying. At this stage it is still perfectly drinkable, but these types of aromas constitute the veil covering the subtler aspects of the sake. As *namazake* gets worse, the veil thickens to a curtain and then a veritable wall. If things are permitted to progress too much, the sake will become cloudy in appearance and yeasty and cheesy in aromas. This condition is called *hi-ochi,* and the sake is undrinkable, to say the least.

The cloudiness in *namazake* gone bad is different from that of regular *nigorizake.* In *nigori,* the sediment will settle, whereas in bad *nama* it will float suspended throughout, often in visible strands. That would be your cue to avoid it.

For the record, I am not anti-*nama.* Not at all! I am, if anything, pro-clarification. In the final analysis, any sake—*nama* or pasteurized—is in the palate of the beholder. *Namazake* can be wonderful. But it is not better than pasteurized sake, at least not simply by virtue of just being *nama.*

Aged Sake

Sake should be consumed while still young; you do not want to collect it, lay it down, or age it. Generally, the sooner after purchasing you drink it, the better.

But there are exceptions. There are *always* exceptions in the sake world.

In truth, the above is the conventional logic. Almost always, sake is best enjoyed young and fresh. Certainly some brewers will mature their product before shipping it to the market, often upward of two years. But once it gets to you, they expect you to enjoy it relatively soon, and not age it any longer.

However, aged sake does exist. There are products out there that are three-, five-, and ten-year-aged sake, and occasionally even older. Aged sake can be very, very interesting. But it is an extremely small part of the market. Most brewers do not make any aged sake at all. It is very much a niche sector and will likely always remain so. But because it holds great potential for engaging enjoyment, it is well worth understanding thoroughly.

I am usually quite reticent to broach the topic of aged sake. It is expensive, hard to find, a totally different animal from regular sake, and most definitely not a better way to do things—it's just different. The methodology is a hassle to grasp, as there are many variables involved and different ways to mature. Even just how aged sake turns out is far too varied to convey concisely. Perhaps the biggest reason I am wary to promote aged sake is that sometimes people like to latch on to the rare, the expensive, and the special. This presents a problem because so little aged sake exists. If people come to like it because of its rarity, perceived value, or even price, then when they find they can get so little of it, they may leave it behind and move on to—God forbid!—another premium beverage. I would much prefer folks come to know and appreciate aged sake gradually, by going *through* the world of orthodox sake, and not around it.

Still, while I may shy away from actively promoting aged sake, I am fascinated by it and enjoy it immensely. Should you pursue sake connoisseurship, aged sake is eventually a must-study.

Although some aged sake has always existed—records of it go back to the 13th century—young sake has always been what most people drank and comprised most of what was produced. But back in the late 1800s, when the modern-day laws governing sake were written,

Daruma Masamune Junen Koshu

SHIRAKI TSUNESUKE SHOTEN GK, GIFU

Maple, spice, and earth in the aromas; butterscotch, prunes, and prominent acidity in the flavor. The quintessential aged sake profile.

Daruma Masamune has based their existence on *koshu* and made a brand out of aging sake. Almost everything they make is aged, and they are the leader in established, consistent, enjoyable, and well-marketed *koshu*. There is a wide range of small-portion sets and gifts, including an arrangement of three-year, five-year, and ten-year sake, which makes the progression sake goes through as it ages easy to understand.

sake brewers were taxed on the amount of sake they brewed. Taxes were collected regularly, whether or not the product had been sold. As such, while not illegal, there was very little motivation to wait several years to sell product on which tax had already been paid. Nor was there much interest in aging product and seeing how it turned out, since if it did not sell, the brewer would lose revenue as well as the tax paid. So, by and large, aged sake ceased to exist.

The law changed in the late 1940s, and brewers began to be taxed on what was sold, not what was brewed. Soon after that, a handful—just a handful, mind you—of brewers began to experiment with aging sake. But even today, most brewers do not mess with it, and way less than 1 percent of all sake is aged any significant length of time.

Possibly because it is a comparatively recent thing, just how a sake is aged varies hugely. For example, sake can be aged at cool cellar temperatures, or at any one of several lower temperatures via refrigeration. It can be aged in steel brewing tanks, small glass bottles, or even ceramic vessels of various sizes. It can be matured for varying lengths of time ranging from two to twenty years. Each one of these choices imparts a different character to the sake.

Also, the type of sake a brewer starts with greatly affects the outcome, naturally enough. A light *daiginjo* made with highly milled rice will mature much differently from a rich *junmai* with its heavy, amino-acid-laden flavor. Not only the milling rate but the added alcohol, the original acidity, the original sugar and amino acid content, and other factors will affect how a sake matures.

As you can imagine, with the myriad of possible combinations of aging and ingredients, how aged sake will taste is all over the map. For example, a light and dry *daiginjo* matured for five years at refrigerated temperatures in the bottle might just end up with a more well-rounded flavor—and be vastly improved by that. The other extreme would see a rich *jun-mai* made with rice milled much less, and then aged in tanks for ten years. This would surely be earthy, almost musty perhaps, rich and umami-laden, and quite amber in color to boot.

In general, this is what happens to sake: it takes on color, earthiness, and richness, and the acidity can become more prominent as well. Often, sake matures in much the way that a sherry matures. But it is important to remember that the results will vary greatly depending on the conditions of both brewing and storage.

There are a couple of terms that refer to aged sake. The simplest is *koshu*, which means "old" sake. However, the nuance of this term is such that it can imply something left lying around, i.e., sake that has been inadvertently aged. As such, to refer to sake that has been deliberately matured, the term *choki-jukusei-shu* is more common. The bigger term belies its bigger flavors, but perhaps that is just a coincidence.

Note that an official vintage system does not exist in the sake world. There are two reasons for this. One is that most sake is not aged. A vintage year is hard to speak about when there is no product. Second, the goal of most sake producers is consistency from year to year for a given product. There is no need for a system that vaunts the merits of a particular year when the goal is continuity of style. However, one does see the word "vintage" on sake labels sometimes, although it just indicates aged sake rather than any existing vintage system.

When brewers age sake, they often refer to its age by using the year in which it was brewed. This year does not, however, correspond with a calendar year.

Because sake is brewed in the cold part of the year (beginning in autumn and finishing the following spring), any given brewing season will straddle two calendar years. Brewers refer to a given BY, or "brewing year," which is a one-year period that begins July 1 and ends June 30 of the following year. As an example, "2013 BY" would begin on July 1, 2013, and end on June 30, 2014. A sake brewed in November 2013 and one brewed in April 2014 would both be part of "2013 BY." This ensures that all the sake labeled with a given BY was made in the same brewing season.

As complicated as it might seem here, it makes great sense in the sake-brewing world.

Of course, it is possible to experiment and age sake yourself. You would learn a lot and might even like the result. But what you would *not* be doing is enjoying your sake the way the brewer intended you to enjoy it, as it would have become a different sake altogether. But it might be worth that sacrifice to learn firsthand how sake matures.

While it seems best for the burgeoning world of sake appreciation outside Japan that we all focus on the 99 percent of the market that is orthodox young sake, aged sake has its immense appeal as well. It's not better than young sake, just different, but well worth the effort to learn about.

The *Nihonshu-do*

There is such a thing as "too much information." Often, in an attempt to be helpful to consumers, or in an effort to make things seem more interesting, the industry disseminates data of dubious usefulness, which just confuses, or worse, intimidates. I think the *nihonshu-do* is one such culprit.

The *nihonshu-do* is often translated into English as the "Sake Meter Value," a direct translation that works fine. Often abbreviated SMV on English-language labels, it is a number associated with a sake that is supposed to indicate sweetness or dryness, but in reality it does not. At least not very well.

The *nihonshu-do* is usually between −2 and +10 for most sake, although it could be much higher or lower. Just remember "higher is dryer": the higher the number, the dryer the sake, and the lower the number, the sweeter the sake. More or less.

Sake Meter Value actually refers to the density of the sake compared to the density of pure water and is measured with an instrument called a hydrometer. A measurement of zero does not indicate "neutral" in terms of sweet and dry, but rather a density equal to that of water.

Although the number we see on the label, when it's provided, gives us an approximation of the sugar content of the sake, this alone will not tell us much about how sweet or dry the sake tastes. Therein lies the problem.

There are a handful of other aspects of a sake that will affect the overall sensation of

sweet and dry, and each one of these will contribute a certain percentage of error. Let's look
at a few of these.

First, consider acidity, which can make
a sake taste drier. Between two sake with the
same *nihonshu-do*, the one with the higher acidity will taste drier. This effect can be significant
and can induce perhaps a 25 percent error to
the *nihonshu-do* reading.

Next let's look at temperature, which can
make our perceptions of sweet and dry vary
hugely. For many people sweetness becomes
more noticeable at warmer temperatures,
at least to a certain point. A sake might taste
entirely different in terms of sweetness and dryness when tasted chilled versus at room temperature or warmer. This might also impart a
25 percent error.

Naturally, the food with which we enjoy
a sake will have its say as well. Oversimplifying just a bit, a saltier dish or snack will bring
out an apparent sweetness in a given sake. Add
another 25 percent error on for this.

And, of course, there is personal taste. What
one person considers sweet in a sake might not
be so for the next person. Also, if you taste several sake, what you tasted just a moment ago can
affect what you sense afterward. After a bone-
dry sake, for example, anything else will taste
sweet by comparison. Tack on another 50 percent error for these two factors.

Arguably, aromatics also affect things.
When sensing apple, banana, or melon in the
aromas of a *ginjo*, for example, we tend to think
sweet rather than dry. And when a sake is *nama*
(unpasteurized) the attendant aromas very
commonly mislead people into thinking a sake
is sweeter. Here again we might see a 25 percent error imposed.

Considering the above factors, we have a
combined potential error of 150 percent, which
basically means the *nihonshu-do* is wrong all the
time, and then some.

Hyperbole aside, the point is that the *nihonshu-do* is by itself not a very accurate measurement of anything, much less sweet or dry. But that is not to say it is a totally useless number. A practical way to use it is to remember that *in its extreme manifestations* the *nihonshu-do* is a measurement of sweet and dry. A +10 will come across as dry to anyone; a −2 will seem sweet. But in between those extremities, the *nihonshu-do* is fairly useless.

In truth, it was never meant for public consumption. As mentioned above, it is a hydrometer reading and has a mathematical correlation to hydrometer readings used in making wine and beer. It is a technical tool used during the brewing process, a measurement that tells the brewer how both starch-to-sugar and sugar-to-alcohol conversions are proceeding. Each sake will have a target number as the final *nihonshu-do*, but that is really just one facet of a wide

Harushika Junmai Chokarakuchi

IMANISHI SEIBEI SHOTEN, NARA

A decidedly prominent astringency defines the aroma. Extremely dry, but with a rich viscosity. A great pairing with bacon-sprinkled cream-based pasta.

The *kura* is one of the oldest breweries in Nara, once in charge of making sake for the famous Shinto shrine Kasuga Jinja. *Chokarakuchi* means "super dry," and the +12 is an example of a *nihonshu-do* level that is indeed worth paying attention to. The average for sake these days is about +4; a glance at the label on this product will let you know for sure that it is quite dry.

range of factors and decisions that go into making a sake what it is.

Somewhere along the line, some brewers began to put this information on labels, and after a while it became laden with undue importance.

Putting the *nihonshu-do* on the label is neither required nor regulated. Rarely is it listed on the label for anything but premium sake, and even then it is listed perhaps half the time. No one really hides the number from the public (it is available for almost any sake on the internet, should you want to work that hard), but many do not consider the *nihonshu-do* relevant information for customers.

I myself never actively look for it, yet neither would I shield my eyes should it come into my field of vision when scanning a label. It's just not that important, that's all.

The average *nihonshu-do* these days is about +4. This is a solid and strong average because many, many sake's *nihonshu-do* values congregate around that figure. This is yet another reason I find it somewhat undependable.

An ostensibly better measurement for assessing sweet and dry has been developed in Japan using a mathematical combination of the *nihonshu-do* and the measured acidity together. While this holds minimally better potential for indicating sweet or dry, it has not been enthusiastically embraced (read: no one is using it).

Perhaps the main point here is that although the *nihonshu-do* is interesting and readily available information, it is best to not place too much importance on it. It is certainly not worth factoring into a decision on which sake to choose. Sweet or dry may be something to consider, but to reiterate, the *nihonshu-do* alone will not tell you much about that except in its extreme manifestations.

So how are we to know, then? Just taste it! Most sake is not extreme in sweetness, dryness, or any other aspect. There are countless aspects of a sake that are more prominent and important than sweetness or a lack thereof.

Ask about a sake, take a chance, taste and smell it for yourself, and note your observations. Not only is this the best way, it is surely the only dependable way to assess a sake. For better or worse, nothing on the label will tell you very much about what awaits you inside.

Ginjo

"If you remember one word about sake, let that word be *ginjo*. *Ginjo* sake is super-premium sake; if you drink something with the word *ginjo* written somewhere on the label, you will be drinking a sake in the top 10 percent of all sake made."

I cannot tell you how many times I have intoned those words, directed at people interested in sake who want to start to enjoy it immediately and without undue effort. As overly simplistic as it might seem, I stand by that line. It works; it achieves its purpose. People walk away from a seminar or article and can walk into a restaurant, pub, or retailer and sound like sake cognoscenti, or at least not have to worry about sounding foolish. At the same time they can order or buy sake and know that the chances of being disappointed are slim. The formula makes sake approachable to the masses and brings into the fold folks who might otherwise never try sake.

So I stand by that line.

But it ain't the entire truth. In fact, it ain't even close.

Here, the word *ginjo* refers to all four subclasses of this grade: *ginjo* and *junmai ginjo*, and the even better duo of *daiginjo* and *junmai daiginjo* (just remember that *daiginjo* is "*ginjo* to die for"). Recall that if the word *junmai* is *not* there, some alcohol has been added as an accepted part of the process. (See the chapter on *junmai* vs. non-*junmai* on page 25, for more.) Mildly confusing nomenclature though it may be, these four types together are collectively called *ginjo* or *ginjo-shu*. Indeed, *ginjo* sake makes up about 10 percent of the market today. And yes, it is super premium, it is great stuff, and it is generally more expensive than other grades of sake. But it is not the only grade of sake worth drinking, and it's not everyone's first choice.

Why in the world would the technically best stuff not be what everyone wants to drink? Because it is a classification that has its own style and nature, and that might not be what appeals to everyone, or what appeals at all times. In other words, *ginjo* can be light, delicate, and aromatic, low in acidity and earthiness. Not all *ginjo*, mind you—some are plenty rich and earthy. But in general, as a style, *ginjo* is aromatic and delicate. Yes, it calls for great technical skill, expensive rice that has been highly milled, and more time and effort to produce, hence the higher price tag. Nevertheless, there are those

Kidoizumi Hyakugokko "Fragrant Jewel" Nama Junmai Yamahai

KIDOIZUMI SHUZO KK, CHIBA

Bold, rich fruit and acid in both aromas and flavor. Big and juicy, with banana, citrus, gamey rice, and acid to finish.

This brewery has refused to jump on the more-milling-is-better bandwagon. Some *kura* make only cheap sake and therefore no *ginjo*; here, they make great, creative, and diverse types of sake—just no *ginjo-shu*. They are remarkably successful with several unique types of sake, including this *yamahai* and a series of aged sake called AFS.

who prefer sake that is more big-boned, earthy, or less aromatic.

"*Ginjo*, schminjo," they say.

One side of this argument is the nature of *ginjo* itself. Many say *ginjo* will "tire you out," or that the aromatics are cloying. Some folks prefer more of a workingman's sake, like a *junmai-shu* or even a *honjozo*. Especially when planning to sit down and drink several glasses, some find that *ginjo*—and even more so, *daiginjo*—have aromatics that can be overpowering after the first glass. Not all, but some. Some sake aficionados feel lower grades tend to make better session sake. Not all, but some.

It may be too that preferences change with age, as they are wont to do. Many of the "*ginjo*, schminjo" adherents seem to be older gentlemen. My own preferences have gravitated toward less ostentatious sake over the last quarter century. *Ginjo*, schminjo may be a natural progression in life.

The other side of the coin is just how interesting, worthwhile, and enjoyable it can be to drink sake of other grades. When I first got into sake, I got *way* into *ginjo*, and it was all I was interested in trying. In fact, as I spent time with brewers and other industry types, I was chided for this more than once. "You just went straight for the *ginjo* there, didn't ya!" I'd be told, lightly implying that I was an inexperienced simpleton.

That good-natured joking had a positive effect and encouraged me to expand my sake horizons. Also, over time I realized that the best way to learn about any given brewer or region was to taste as wide a range of types as possible. *Honjozo* sake can be surprisingly wonderful; *futsu-shu* can teach more about the regional styles of sake than most other grades. It is all worth trying and drinking. Limiting oneself to *ginjo* is cutting off 90 percent of the wonders of the world of sake.

Surely there are those with *ginjo*-phobia.

Some codgers don't really know what makes *ginjo* what it is, what defines it, and what makes it special, and I count many an aforementioned older gentleman among that number. Rather than take the time to learn about it, or hint at anything less than a complete understanding of the sake world, they stick with what they know, be it *honjozo* or another non-*ginjo* grade, and recite the mantra "*ginjo*, schminjo."

Don't get me wrong: I love *ginjo*. It can be outstanding and is the pinnacle of the brewer's craft. I enjoy plenty of it. All I am saying is while it is okay to immediately gravitate toward *ginjo* to check it out, by all means don't limit yourself to only sake of that grade.

I recall being at one promotional tasting overseas, and up came a woman who asked for the most expensive *daiginjo* we were pouring. In fact, I had heard her ask the same thing of the brewer next to me. "I only drink the best," she explained with conviction. Before I had a chance to ask "In whose opinion?" or "Based on what criteria?" she had scampered off to the next "best" one down the line, presumably the next *daiginjo*.

If it tastes good to you to you, it is good. The one that tastes the best to you is the best.

Ginjo, schminjo.

Sake Purity

Is it gluten free? Is it vegan?

Sake is often hailed for its purity. After all, it is made from rice, *koji* mold, and water. Oh, and much of it is made with the addition of some pure, distilled ethyl alcohol. However, no preservatives are used, sake is sulfite free, and once the brewing process is completed nothing can be added but water and *kasu* (see page 64).

But is sake gluten free? And is it vegan? These are growing concerns these days, and sake holds great potential as something that people with these concerns can enjoy.

The short answer to both is "Yes, sake is both gluten free and vegan." However, the truth is that it is not feasible to absolutely, 100 hundred percent guarantee that all sake made everywhere at any time conforms to these restrictions. But for almost all people and situations, we can say yes, it conforms to both.

Let's start with the question of gluten. Sake is brewed rice; rice is the only grain used and the only fermentable material. Rice does not contain any gluten. So far, so good. The only other ingredients are water, *koji* mold (*Aspergillus oryzae*), and yeast. If a sake uses only these ingredients—as all *junmai* sake types do—then yes, we can say that it is absolutely gluten free. Done. Quod erat demonstrandum.

If glutens are a concern, drink something with the word *junmai* on the label, because that is a gluten-free sake.

But what about the non-*junmai* types? What of *futsu-shu*, *honjozo*, and the non-*junmai* *ginjo* and *daiginjo* grades? These have had a bit of pure distilled alcohol added. From where does this alcohol come? Can this be said to be gluten-free too?

First things first: Psst! It's ethyl alcohol! The chemical formula is C_2H_6O. Regardless of its source, the alcohol added to sake has been distilled over and over so that it is nothing more than ethyl alcohol, at least in my thinking. However, this might not satisfy some people.

Next, let's look at the source. Almost without exception, the alcohol added to non-*junmai* sake is cheap and imported, having been distilled from sugar cane, which contains no gluten. I'm aware of a couple whacked-out (in a good way) brewers who actually distill alcohol from their own (gluten-free) *junmai-shu* and add that to their products.

I cannot say with airtight certainty that no brewer anywhere ever uses alcohol distilled from barley or another gluten-containing

Kikusui Organic Junmai Ginjo

KIKUSUI SHUZO KK, NIIGATA

Subtle banana and melon notes augmented by an earthy acidity in the aromas and a comparatively full volume to the flavor; overall dry and straightforward.

The brewery grows certified organic rice in the U.S. and ships it back to Japan. The sake brewed with that rice is then shipped back overseas. There are a handful of breweries making organic sake in Japan, but only Kikusui goes to this degree to engage organic sake fans abroad. Note: This sake is *only* available in the U.S.

grain. This should not matter as—unlike whiskey—the alcohol has been distilled to the point that only ethyl alcohol remains. But there is no guarantee that it was not barley once upon a time.

However, I can *almost* guarantee it, for a very clear reason.

Sugar cane–based ethyl alcohol is extremely cheap, whereas barley-based ethyl alcohol is expensive. No brewer in his or her right mind is going to pay any more than he or she has to for this stuff. Economically it would make no sense for a brewer to use anything but the cheapest variety, since it is chemically identical. So, although there is no absolute guarantee that non-*junmai* sake is gluten-free, there practically is, because the cheapest alcohol comes from sugar cane, not barley.

Finally, consider *futsu-shu*, the cheapest sake, made with both added alcohol and sometimes sugars. Here we might have a problem! That sweetening agent may have been from rice-based *koji*, in which case we are fine. But there is a chance that the sweetening agent was *mizu-ame*, which is mostly made from an extra-starchy rice called *mochigome*. Some barley-based malt *may* have also been added to get the starch-to-sugar conversion going. Just a bit, mind you, but not zero.

The point here is that some *futsu-shu* has sweeteners added to it. Some of that is from rice-based *koji*. But we cannot tell from the label the source of these sugars, so it is possible that the *futsu-shu* was made with a *minuscule* amount of barley.

One more caution: What of fruit-flavored or other flavored sake? What about the added flavorings? Can we say that those are gluten free?

In Japan, fruit flavors cannot be added to sake. Once you do, the product is no longer legally sake. It is not a purist thing, it is a legal and tax thing. So no fruit-flavored sake exists in

Japan (this includes popular sake-based *ume-shu*, or plum "sake," which many think is sake but legally is not). However, these laws do not apply to fruit-flavored sake made in other countries. Certainly, the producers would have the necessary information for those who need to confirm whether these sakes are indeed gluten free.

What about sake being vegan? This one may prove a bit trickier, or, as they say, "It's complicated."

No animal products of any type are used in the production of sake. However, after sake has been brewed, it is usually filtered with charcoal, and some breweries then use an animal-based gelatin to help remove the charcoal. This does not end up in the final sake, but it is used at some stage of the process.

Most brewers do *not* do this, but one cannot easily tell from the label. Also, not all sake is charcoal filtered. If a sake has not been charcoal filtered, then the gelatin would not have been used. Sake that has not been charcoal filtered is known as *muroka*.

If a sake is of the *junmai* variety, we can say that it conforms to vegan standards because only rice, water, and *koji* mold were used.

This leads us to one safe haven: if a sake is a *junmai*, *junmai ginjo*, or *junmai daiginjo*, and if it is *muroka*, then yes, that sake is vegan.

If a sake is not a *junmai* type, in other words, if a bit of alcohol was added during the process, it would still be vegan since nothing involved in distilling the added alcohol would disqualify it. But in the end it would still depend on whether or not animal-based gelatin was also used.

There is one more caveat: lactic acid is used in the production of most sake. But such lactic acid is industrially produced from lactic bacteria, not from animal sources. This also applies to any lacto-sugars that might be used as well; they are not animal based.

In summary: anything with the word *junmai* on the label is sure to be gluten free. Any premium sake is almost certain to be. *Futsu-shu* may be dodgy, but you don't likely want to drink much *futsu-shu* anyway.

Any sake that is not charcoal filtered (*muroka*, but this is not always indicated on the label) is sure to be vegan. Only the very few that use animal-based gelatin would not be vegan, so even non-*junmai* sake could be vegan too. However, we cannot know from the label if such gelatins were used.

While the above may not be as clear-cut or as simple as we would like it to be, most sake is *highly likely* to be both gluten free and vegan, although this cannot be absolutely guaranteed.

The Date on the Bottle and "How Long Is Too Long?"

Freshness is important! When it comes to sake, while "the fresher the better" might be a little bit of an exaggeration, we still need to know how old a given bottle might be. The information we can garner from the label will not tell us everything—far from it! But usually it is enough, and in any event is very worth understanding.

Sake bottles do have a date on them, usually in the lower corner of the label. But what is this date? The day on which the sake was born, or on which brewing was completed? Is it the best-enjoyed-by date, perhaps? It is actually something else altogether. And not surprisingly, it is shrouded in vagueness.

For all intents and purposes, the date on the bottle is the date that the sake was shipped from the *kura*. The key phrase here is *for all intents and purposes*.

In actuality, brewers legally must affix the date when the sake is bottled, with the thinking being that they will ship it soon after bottling it. This is the way things had long been done: store it in a tank, bottle it just before shipping, and pay taxes on it. And make no mistake, it is really all about taxes. But I digress.

So, if a sake is dated when bottled, but bottled just before it is shipped, then for all intents and purposes the date can be considered to be the shipping date. However, some sake are not shipped just after bottling. If a brewer bottles in huge lots, for example, some might go out that day but the rest might not go out for months. Some sake will fall through the cracks of those intents and purposes.

However, more and more commonly, sake is stored in bottles rather than tanks; this is especially true for premium sake. Many brewers feel this gives sake a more fine-grained and delicate texture. So the rules have been bent to read that the date must be applied when you bottle the sake, unless you plan to age it in that bottle. In that case, the brewer is not permitted to label the bottle. The date is applied when the sake comes out of maturation and is labeled.

This means that when a sake is aged in a bottle and is taken out of storage, labeled, dated, and finally shipped, then for all intents and purposes the date can be considered to be the shipping date. Or at least, that's how I see it.

So, the date on the bottle is the bottling date. Unless it isn't.

This is why I prefer the *for all intents and purposes* addendum, and hold that the date on a bottle of sake indicates about when (month and year) the sake was shipped from the *kura*.

Note, too, what this date does *not* tell you. It does not tell you how old the sake is. Different brewers mature sake for different periods of time to achieve the desired flavor profile. A brewer of a lighter sake might mature it for only four months or so, but a brewer of a more earthy style might have the sake sit for a year and a half before shipping. Either way, they want you to enjoy it immediately since they matured it to just where they want it. But both might have the same date on the bottle and be over a year apart since being brewed.

The date also does not tell you if the sake was aged in a bottle or a tank, or how long it was aged at all. Nor does it tell you how much time you have before you can expect noticeable changes to the flavor, or by when you should drink it. That date is nothing but the bottling date. Unless it isn't.

Since we know that we cannot trust that date to tell us much, how old is too old? How soon after the printed date should we consume a sake to be assured it is fresh and in prime drinking condition? As much as I know that everyone wants a straight, short, and clear answer, there isn't one.

Just how long is too long depends on a whole host of things. How was the sake shipped? In a refrigerated container? (Almost all sake is these days.) How was it stored when it got to its destination? In a warm-ish warehouse or a refrigerated one? How much time since it left the *kura* has been spent under the bright lights of the retailer?

Then there is the sake itself to consider. Is it a style that will stand up to maturation or

Mori no Kura "Gen Enjuku" Junmai Ginjo

KK MORINOKURA, FUKUOKA

Slightly amber in color with cocoa and brown sugar aromas followed by flavors in a similar vein, rich and full. Room temperature or even gently warmed is where this sake really opens up.

This *kura* brews several lines of sake, and while not all are mature styles, this product is. As it will see four to five years of tank maturation before bottling, it is a great example of how the bottle date is no indication of how old the sake actually is. A sticker on the neck boldly proclaims the year it was brewed, clearing up any potential confusion in advance.

not? Some sake will change much less than other sake over the same time period and under the same storage conditions. Alcohol content, acidity, whether it is *junmai* or non-*junmai*, and the milling rate all affect this. As an example, a robust sake with a slightly higher-than-normal acidity and even a slightly higher-than-usual alcohol will last much longer than a light, delicate, aromatic *daiginjo*. A dry sake will exhibit much less change than a sake with more glucose and amino acid content.

What cannot be said about sake in general, or even any one sake, is that after a certain number of days, weeks, or months, a sake is automatically and definitely "too old." If I had to give a short answer, a rule of thumb, I would say sake is good for no more than eighteen months. Still, take this with a grain of salt, and don't consider it a hard-and-fast number. This rule assumes the producer is good and the importer is conscientious enough to have stored it properly.

So what should you do if you are not sure? Taste it. With enough tasting experience, you can learn to taste when sake is too old. You can do this by deliberately aging sake and seeing what happens to it, but perhaps it is better to taste sake that you know has gotten old. Learn how too much time in a bottle manifests itself in sake and apply that knowledge. That is the surest—and most enjoyable—way to know "How old is too old?"

Everyone wants one straight, short answer. But it doesn't exist. That is the truth.

THE TRUTH ABOUT

Warm Sake

The "hot versus cold" dichotomy may be one of sake's biggest distractions. Many people are unsure which is the right choice for which sake, and why that is. Add to that the questions of how one can tell, how to warm the sake, and the inevitable complexities that come along with personal preferences, and it can all be daunting.

This is why many sake promoters have oversimplified things by polarizing the answer into "good sake should be chilled, bad sake can be heated." Not only is it not that simple, but that statement is not even close to being correct.

It is true that historically, if not tradition-ally, more sake was served warm than cold. His-torical records and vessels show that sake was enjoyed warm as far back as the 10th century. It is very likely that the practice made it to Japan via neighboring China, where eating and drinking warmed things has always been con-sidered healthier than eating cold things, which were thought to chill the center of the body.

However, as premium sake like *ginjo* devel-oped into more aromatic, delicate stuff (in per-haps the late 1980s), the concept of enjoying premium sake slightly chilled gained momen-tum. Why? Because heating sake like that would bludgeon out of existence the traits that the brewers worked so hard to draw out. The practice of chilling premium sake caught on in Japan, and by the '90s, it seemed that premium warm sake was beginning to be forgotten. Or at least it was awaiting rediscovery.

This trend played into what was hap-pening overseas as well. While sake importers strove to capture the hearts and palates of the wine-loving world, they often met a brick wall.

"I've had sake. No thanks. Not interested."

"Ah," would come the reply. "But have you had premium sake, like *ginjo*? It is served cold, not hot, and I guarantee you it is different from what you have had before!" This ploy would get folks to taste sake, and often, to appreciate it, so it has served a purpose.

But this led to an all-too-familiar and over-simplified perception that good sake should be enjoyed cold, and less-good sake should be drunk hot. While enjoying premium sake slightly chilled can still be a useful rule of thumb for those just getting into sake, the fact that there is almost no bad sake in existence anymore renders the second half of the statement moot.

Perhaps the most egregious of untruths (misconceptions?) out there is that bad sake is heated to cover the flaws. There has never been a brewer that tasted his product, looked around, and said, "Woah, this stuff is *bad*. Let's heat it and fool everyone." Nah, I don't think so. Sake is not now—nor has it ever been—heated to deliberately cover the flaws. Surely heating will accomplish that to some degree, but it was never the objective of warming.

Why then is hot sake everywhere, at every Japanese restaurant around? Why does it seem to be the go-to sake? Part of the reason is that only a very small share of the market is the kind of sake that would suffer from warming. The majority of all sake made is still simple, straight-forward "table sake." Remember, just because something isn't fruity doesn't mean it isn't good. *Ginjo*, schminjo, say some.

So, in one sense, warming is more of a tra-ditional way to enjoy sake, and tradition dies hard. And, like any industry, the large players benefit from selling lots of inexpensive product, and much of that is enjoyed hot simply because it always has been. Also, *ginjo* has only been around as a significant presence in the market since the early '80s. Much more sake before that period was indeed suited to warming. All of these factors combined have helped hot sake to maintain its presence.

While the generalization that most *ginjo* is best enjoyed slightly chilled serves a purpose, the truth is deliciously more complex, interesting, and appealing.

Warming a sake that has a flavor profile suited to it can lead to a life-altering experience. Much of this epiphany-inducing sake is premium *ginjo*. So, yes, there are *ginjo* that can be warmed with delicious results.

What makes a *ginjo*—or any other sake— suited to warming is nothing more than the flavor profile. Very often an earthiness—perhaps characterized by higher bitterness, acidity, or even sweetness, but more importantly the combination of these—lets a sake meld into something extraordinary when warmed. But it need

Kamoizumi "Shusen" Junmai Ginjo

KAMOIZUMI SHUZO KK, HIROSHIMA

A captivating blend of sweetness, richness, and earthiness that is consistent across the aromas and flavors.

While most of Hiroshima Prefecture is known for its soft water, Kamoizumi is brewed in an area known as Saijo that sits over a narrow strip of hard-water wells, giving a fullness to the sake from the handful of *kura* there. While this sake is perfectly enjoyable at room temperature, it really opens up and comes into its own and becomes decidedly much better when gently or even thoroughly warmed. Don't be shy with this one.

not be complex: dry, thick, and/or umami-laden sake can morph into something wonderfully different at warm temperatures too.

How can one tell? Often in Japan the producer will indicate recommended serving temperatures on the label, but this information rarely appears on exported product, probably because the importer—rather than the producer—wants to keep things simple for the customer. In terms of styles, *yamahai* and *kimoto* types (see page 76) as well as sake with some maturity are naturals as candidates for warming.

In truth, the best way to know is trial and error. Try a sake—any sake that you enjoy—at room temperature rather than chilled. Then take the ones that appealed to you at room temperature and try them a bit warmer. There are no rules except the ones that are constantly being broken anyway.

The advantage to doing things this way is that you will also discover one of the best secrets: any one given sake will be enjoyable as a different animal at each temperature range. Sure, each one will have a temperature at which it tastes best to you on that day and in that situation. But its appeal across a range of temperatures will fascinate you. Even just "hot" and "cold" are tremendously limiting. Long ago, there were a dozen words in Japanese used to refer to the wide range of temperatures at which sake might be served. These days, though, very few are used with any regularity.

Warm or hot sake is known generically as *kanzake* or *o-kan*. *Atsukan* means piping-hot sake, whereas *nurukan* refers to more tepid sake, an absolutely wonderful if vague temperature range for enjoying premium sake.

Then there is the *how* of warming sake. Is there one best way? Of course not! But one principle worth remembering is that sake should be heated by immersing a vessel of choice into just-boiled or simmering water and stirring occasionally for a few minutes until it reaches the desired temperature, which is verified empirically (read: taste the stuff as you warm it). It is best not to do it in water that is actively boiling as that can cause some of the alcohol to evaporate, skewing the original make-up of the sake. A microwave oven will work in a pinch, but it is hard to be accurate, and this method also seems to rob the sake of some character (although there are no scientific grounds for this).

There seems to be a modern renaissance in Japan over warmed sake, and the tools, toys, and accoutrements available these days are both fun and practical. Many are cheap, simple devices that fit a sake-containing vessel into another that holds hot water, like a miniature double boiler, which warms sake predictably and consistently. These are well worth the search!

★ ★ ★

I, too, was once a chilled *ginjo* snob. When I first got into premium sake, for several years I drank nothing but *ginjo*, and never any way but chilled. As I spent more time with brewers, though, I was often chided for my lack of imagination.

"Listen, kid," I recall being told. "You wanna know what a good sake is? A good sake is one that can be enjoyed *both* chilled *and* warm. Now *that's* a good sake!" I figured I was not one to argue with someone who had been in this industry several generations longer than me, so I took the words to heart. Man, am I glad I did.

Nigori

It seems that everywhere you go, any restaurant (outside of Japan, anyway) that carries sake has at least one *nigorizake* selection. How do they make it and to what does it owe its apparent popularity?

Nigorizake is cloudy sake; in fact, that is what the word *nigori* means. (As with *namazake*, the *s* of "sake" becomes a *z*. And often the suffix *-zake* is dropped in conversation.) Those clouds within, the sediment, is made up of particles of rice that did not or could not ferment and were permitted into the final product.

Long ago, all sake was *nigori*. Until perhaps a thousand years ago, no one bothered to separate the completed sake from the rice particles after fermentation. Records reveal a couple of different stories of what happened to change this.

One version is that a brewery in the erstwhile brewing capital of Itami, in modern-day Hyogo Prefecture, fired one its employees. The disgruntled and now jobless brewer snuck back into the *kura* and, as an act of vengeance, dumped copious amounts of powdered charcoal into a tank of just-completed, white sake. "That'll show 'em!" he likely thought.

Oh, it showed 'em all right. It showed them how to make clear sake. The charcoal dragged down the rice particles, and when the brewers pressed that through a mesh to try to save it, voila! They had clear sake, and that soon became the norm. Or so goes the story.

However, in nearby Nara Prefecture, there are records that show that the monks who primarily brewed in temples were selling sake *kasu*, the white cakes of rice particles that are the by-product of the pressing process, or passing the sake through a mesh. Sake *kasu* is used in making pickles and in other traditional food.

The monks in Nara have records of selling this stuff long before the charcoal-dumping event in Itami. If they were selling *kasu*, they had to have been pressing their sake before Itami.

Regardless of who started making *nigori*, almost all sake today is clear.

Nigorizake is often referred to as "unfiltered sake," and that is a perfectly good term. But because completed sake usually involves a second filtration process using either powdered charcoal or a ceramic filter, the first filtration that removes all the rice particles is often referred to as "pressing."

Tsuki no Katsura Junmai Daiginjo Nigorizake

MASUDA TOKUBEE SHOTEN KK, KYOTO

Slightly sweet, spritzy in spite of the copious amounts of rice solids remaining.

The brewers here do make plenty of wonderful orthodox sake, but they are also one of the most significant producers of *nigorizake* in the industry, using the special method they developed in the 1960s. Theirs is one of the few *daiginjo nigori* in existence.

In time, the industry moved toward pressing almost all sake, and clear sake became the norm. However, out in the countryside, rice farmers would make their own sake—illegally of course—and they would not bother to clarify it. So when the sake tax laws were rewritten in the late 1800s, it was stipulated that sake had to "pass through a mesh" before being sold. As a result, for decades, *nigorizake* did not exist as a product genre on the market.

Back in 1966 a very prominent brewery in Kyoto that produces the Tsuki no Katsura brand wanted to begin to make *nigori* in a new and better way. They worked very closely with the Ministry of Taxation, which oversees all these things, to create *nigori* that was legal but still cloudy.

Tokubee Masuda, the owner and president, explained that "it took several months, and at every step, we had to get their buy-in. We would ask, 'If we do it *this* way, it's acceptable, *right*?' Great, now sign off on it please."

What they did was create a cage-like device, an insert with holes in its walls that fit into a tank of sake. The sake that leaked through the holes into the center of the insert was then drawn off and bottled. The government determined that as long as the holes in the mesh were no larger than 2 millimeters in diameter, the result of filtration using the cage could legally be considered sake. Hence, *nigorizake* was born as a genre of sake. Other breweries later followed suit, using their own contraptions. Tsuki no Katsura now makes more *nigorizake* than any *kura* in the country.

So *nigori* came to be sake that is pressed through a coarser mesh that allows some rice particles into the final product. Why is this done? Because it is a fun throwback to moonshine and the way sake was a millennium ago.

As I visited breweries and the topic of *nigori* came up, I would be told from time to time with a smile and in hushed tones that the brewer did not bother to use a special, coarser mesh to make *nigori*.

"We just throw some of the sake *kasu* back into it when we are done. But that is not totally legal, you see . . ."

Well, it seems that I was not the only one being pulled aside and whispered to. Apparently, everyone was doing it that way. And a few years ago, I noticed a change in the wording of the very laws that define sake. It used to be that after pressing, only water could be added to the completed sake. But now, water and *kasu* can be added. It seems that common sense and practicality won out—either that or effective lobbying.

Nigorizake is very popular outside of Japan, and in particular in the U.S. (It is much less popular in Japan.) Why might this be? Some surmise that it is because no matter who brews it, the sake is called *nigori*. And no matter who brews it, it is also white. So it is easy to remember and user friendly.

Nigori can be very enjoyable indeed. It is obviously thicker and more textured, much more viscous than regular sake, more chewy, rice-like, and creamy. However, it can never be as refined as regular sake, nor as light. The rice particles remaining will overpower any subtler nuances of flavor and aroma. As with all things, it is a matter of preference.

For this reason, rarely do we see higher grades of *nigori*, a "*ginjo nigori*," for example. Higher grades are all about increasing refinement. Leaving the dregs goes in the opposite direction. So, while there are in fact a few *nigori* of *ginjo* class out there, most *nigori* is of lower grades.

There are versions of *nigori* called *usu-nigori*, or "thin *nigori*," which is just what it sounds like: *nigorizake* in which only a very small amount of rice dust is allowed to remain. It has a kind of fresh, just-pressed appeal. Very often we see higher *ginjo* grades of sake in this manifestation.

Note also that just because a sake is a *nigori* does not mean it has to taste any one way. There is sweet *nigori*, dry *nigori*, thick *nigori*, and thin *nigori*. Some has visible chunks of rice suspended in it. There is even some *nigori* that is *nama*, although this can be quite unstable.

But it will always be white, and it will always be called *nigori*. In the end, it will always be enjoyable.

Tokubetsu

There are two classifications of sake—*tokubetsu honjozo* and *tokubetsu junmai-shu*—that seem almost buried among the others. Certainly, they are less commonly mentioned, but they are very worthy of the sake connoisseur's attention.

The word *tokubetsu* means "special." Let's consider here just what is so special about special *honjozo* and special *junmai*.

If we look at a chart of sake grades, we see that these two classes sit just below *ginjo-shu* and *junmai ginjo-shu*, and just above *honjozo* and *junmai-shu*. On many less comprehensive charts they are egregiously omitted! But these two grades are bona fide, legally defined grades of sake with full honors, and not just nicknames or terms adopted by some brewers. Sake statisticians (read: the government), however, tend to embed data on these into their statistics on regular *honjozo* and regular *junmai-shu*. Even the government does not give these classifications their due!

Let us start with the actual rules. In order for a sake to be permitted to be labeled as *tokubetsu honjozo* or *tokubetsu junmai*, it must meet at least one of three requirements. One, it is made with rice milled down to 60 percent *seimai-buai* or further. This of course could qualify it as a *ginjo* class. Two, it is made using *shuzo kotekimai*, or proper sake rice. Bear in mind that while almost all premium sake is made using sake rice, most cheap sake is made using run-of-the-mill table rice. Three—and here is where the fun starts—it is special for some other reason, which is supposed to be listed on the label.

In truth, this is as vague as it sounds. If approved by the local tax authorities, a number of methods can be used to make a sake *tokubetsu*. And while the rationale is supposed to be explained on the label, from my experience it not always is. The only concrete example I have ever heard of is a *junmai* that had some *daiginjo* mixed into it. Sake has to be labeled as the lowest grade for which it qualifies, but the mixed-in *daiginjo* made this particular sake special enough to qualify for the term on the label.

However, perhaps 99 percent of the time, a sake labeled as *tokubetsu* will have conformed to either of the first two rules. In other words, almost all *tokubetsu honjozo* and *tokubetsu junmai* are either made with rice milled to *ginjo* levels or made with *shuzo kotekimai*. There are only a few exceptions, and we need not worry about them.

Personally, I think the actual qualifying reason for the *tokubetsu* designation is of secondary importance. Whether due to the milling, the rice, or something else, it is enough for me to know the brewer has ensconced this sake into that class. I will certainly look at all available specs, but just knowing a sake was *tokubetsu* to the brewer is all I need to know before tasting it. In fact, anything beyond that would be distracting to me. I prefer to taste knowing little more than the brewer's intentions or feelings about the sake at hand.

Why in the world would a brewer make a *tokubetsu*? Surely it would be simpler to tweak a sake enough to call it either a *junmai* or a *junmai ginjo*, for example, rather than leave it in the limbo of the *tokubetsu* realm, would it not? The answer lies, as many things do, in marketing.

Let's say a sake brewer has a *junmai-shu* that sells well and has for a long time. And let's say that company has a *junmai ginjo* that also sells well and is perhaps a flagship product. When they want to add a product at a different price point or in a different style, adding another *jun-*

mai or another *junmai ginjo* might be confusing to the market and even detract from the sales of the existing product. So by labeling it *tokubetsu junmai*, they avoid encroaching on either one of their standard products.

This is of course just one example. The motivation often is as simple as coming out with something new and interesting that is delicious and clearly better than the average *junmai-shu* but not quite at the producer's standard for *junmai ginjo*. *Tokubetsu junmai* is a perfect place for something like that.

There are, not surprisingly, comparatively fewer representatives of these grades of sake out there. There are many more full-fledged *junmai-shu*, *junmai ginjo*, *honjozo*, and *ginjo* sake than *tokubetsu junmai* or *tokubetsu honjozo*. But that does not mean the *tokubetsu* sake do not warrant our attention. They most certainly do.

In fact, to me, these two tenuously defined

Murai Tokubetsu Honjozo

MOMOKAWA KK, AOMORI

Citrus-tinged melon aromas, medium-bodied flavor suffused with a mild, creamy, slight sweetness.

This is a textbook example of a great *tokubetsu honjozo* in that it is light and aromatic but not as much as a typical full-fledged *ginjo* often is. The sake qualifies as a *tokubetsu* in each of the two main ways: it is made using 100 percent sake rice, and the rice has been milled to 60 percent, i.e., to *ginjo* levels.

classes offer some of the most enjoyable sake available. On some occasions I have found the *tokubetsu junmai* or even *tokubetsu honjozo* products of a brewer to be eminently more drinkable over the long term than any other product.

Sometimes, regular *junmai-shu* and *honjozo* are almost a smidgen too plebeian for maximum enjoyment. And, once in a while, a *ginjo* sake will taste more like every other *ginjo* out there. As good as that can be, it can seem to be a part of the "*ginjo* borg" collective rather than display the brewer's individuality. So I can occasionally learn much more about a brewer's style by drinking their *tokubetsu junmai* or *tokubetsu honjozo*. Sure, their *daiginjo* might be better sake (according to some standards), but I see more of the brewery, the brewer, and their intentions by drinking these ostensibly lower grades.

However vaguely defined, the two *tokubetsu* classes can exude some of the finer appeal of *ginjo* while maintaining the fuller arrays of richer flavors possible with less highly milled rice. The result can be an exquisite balance. This is why the *tokubetsu* are some of my favorite sake.

THE TRUTH ABOUT
Water

Seminars or conversations about sake often focus on how important the rice is, the effects of milling, and of course that *koji* stuff. And almost inevitably, the talk eventually turns to water. Just how important is it?

My usual response is that water is so important that it goes without saying. While that may seem flippant, I actually sort of mean it. If you don't start with good water, you'll never make good sake. Forget about it. Sake itself is about 80 percent water, and when you include all the water used to wash, soak, and steam as well, about thirty times more water than rice is used to make a batch of sake. So, yes, it's important.

What makes water good? A number of things, but most notably it is a *lack* of things that's important, in particular iron and manganese. Even a very small amount of either of these will adversely affect the taste, smell, and appearance of sake.

There are things that are important to be present, too: elements and compounds like potassium, magnesium, and phosphoric acid that support a healthy environment for the yeast.

One might think it would be easy to fix water these days, to take any source of water and doctor it so that the undesirables are removed and necessary elements are added. Certainly this is possible to some degree. But there is a limit to how much water can be manipulated, and in the end, a source of pure, clean, fermentation-supportive water is indispensable to making even just decent sake.

Japan is blessed with many great sources of

water thanks to the mountains that make up 80 percent of the country's landmass. Most of the water used in sake brewing comes from wells filled with water from snow that has filtered down through these mountains, but there are other sources as well, such as isolated lakes and underground rivers. Many breweries use the water just out of the well as is, while others do some minimal filtering. A few breweries adjust it a bit more after that, but many don't need to go that far.

While good water is everywhere in Japan, some sources are better than others. Naturally, the sake industry has grown up around these. All breweries are where they are because they are over—or near—a great source of water. The main brewing regions—in particular Nada and Fushimi—are located over *huge* sources of great water. Of course, wells do dry up or even become contaminated by pollution or other side effects of industrialization. Once in a great while, they will need to be re-dug. Regions that sit atop plentiful sources of water are able to easily adapt when that need arises.

In the realm of what constitutes good sake-brewing water, there are of course different traits, and the most significant among them is hard water versus soft water. While one is not inherently better than the other, the differences can be profound. Water hardness is defined by the amount of calcium and magnesium in the water; the more there is, the harder the water is. There are chemical measurements that lead to numerical indications of hardness, but the equations yielding these numbers vary a bit from country to country. No matter how hardness is calculated, in the end it is a matter of mineral content.

Different types of water affect sake in different ways. There is, of course, flavor. It is hardly surprising: harder water often leads to sake that is full and impactful on the palate, whereas soft water generally gives rise to sake

73

that is very absorbing and delicate, and perhaps seemingly sweeter. And because water sources do not exist only in their extreme manifestations of hard and soft, there is everything in between as well.

Water hardness also affects fermentation directly. The mineral content of hard water promotes a much more vigorous and faster fermentation, whereas soft water creates a more lackadaisical and slow ferment. While this leads to the generalities of flavor described above, it also means sake can be made much faster with hard water and takes more time with soft water. Conversely, there are those who hold that softer water is better for making *ginjo-shu* as its nature forces a slower process, and the lower temperatures that are used in such conditions can lead to *ginjo*-esque aromas. So while neither is clearly superior, both hard and soft water have their pros and cons.

Sakura Masamune "Ki-ippon" Junmai

SAKURA MASAMUNE KK, HYOGO

Sturdy, earthy, rich with a cleansing acidity at the end. Decidedly not ostentatious, mouth-filling and balanced. Hint of sweetness in flavor.

This company realized hundreds of years ago how water affects sake brewing and is credited with the discovery of Miyamizu, "Shrine Water," the hard water that makes the sake of the Nada region the stuff of legends. The president uses a traditional name handed down over generations, so the current president has been given the same moniker as the original Miyamizu discoverer: Tazaemon Yamamura.

All types of water are found in Japan, from very hard to very soft. However, on most scales, Japan's water is on average slightly softer than that in most of the world. If one were to look at a listing of water hardness for sake breweries around Japan, one would find a large number of them bundled around the "slightly soft" range.

A few famous sources of water have even acquired a bit of a brand. The most well known of these is Miyamizu, or "Shrine Water," which is the source of the very hard water that helped make the Nada region the largest and most significant brewing neighborhood in Japan, historically and currently as well.

While it is romantically tempting to look at water as the "terroir" of sake—something that gives sake its sense of place or ties it to its immediate environment—this is not completely true. The water from a given well may come from within that land, but it was actually sourced in mountains far away and flowed underground to reach its current position. Also, deep in its well, water is not affected at all by what takes place on the surface, such as climate or what naturally grows there. The water is totally independent of that.

And while one source of water is tied to a particular plot of land, so might several other water sources. Hard water from one mountain might fill a well in one corner, while soft water from another range rises up in another well just a short distance away. Once in a while, water is even brought in to replace dried wells or to meet the demands of the brewers. So, yes, while for the most part water from one parcel of land is tied to that land, it is a bit of a stretch to connect water *too* tightly to a sake's sense of place.

The importance of water almost goes without saying, yet there is plenty to be said about it. Be it hard or be it soft, it's got to be good to begin with.

Yamahai and *Kimoto* Sake

Sake made using the *yamahai-shikomi* method or the *kimoto* method are becoming more commonly available and attracting more interest, and this trend will likely continue. Nevertheless, it is hard to find a good, concise explanation of *yamahai* and *kimoto*, much less of their significance. But relax, your search ends here.

To explain what they are and why they are, we need to go back several hundred years. Then, as now, a tank of sake began with a batch of yeast starter (*moto*). Rice, *koji*, and water were all put into a small, waist-high tank. This was then mixed into a puree-like consistency using poles adapted to this purpose. This was rough work and took many hours of repetitive labor to accomplish. It was so tedious that the brewers developed traditional songs to help pass the time, keep awake, and not lose count.

This was for the most part the only method of creating the yeast starter from its inception in the 12th century until the early 20th century, and it came to be known as *kimoto*. Then, in the early 1900s, sake researchers discovered that all that hard mixing work was not really necessary. By adjusting water volume, temperature, and doses of patience, brewers could achieve the same result without the exertion. This method, closely related to the original *kimoto* method in all ways save the physical pole manipulation, took the name *yamahai*. The meaning of this word conveys the cessation of pole pushing, and this is the main difference between the two methods: *kimoto* calls for the tedious mixing with poles, while this is not done in the *yamahai* method.

Let us go off on a tangent for a moment and look at what happens chemically. After a few chemical processes that are beyond the scope of this chapter take place, lactic bacteria fall into the tank from the air. These guys proliferate, and as they do they create lots of lactic acid. This in turn kills other bad bacteria and undesirable yeast and eventually kills the lactic bacteria that begot it. By some miracle of nature for which we should all feel immense gratitude, sake yeast actually like this environment, and they alone can survive in it. So they drop in and proliferate, leading to a healthy yeast starter and eventually a healthy fermentation.

Naturally occurring sake yeast cells floating in the air will drop in when the chemistry invites them; however, today, almost all sake is made by adding carefully selected yeast rather than leaving it to natural selection.

The evolution of sake brewing took a giant leap forward when, just after the *yamahai* method was developed, researchers realized it was all about lactic acid. "Why do we need to wait for the bacteria to create it for us when we can just add it ourselves?" they thought. And so they did, giving rise to the process known as *sokujo-moto*. The word *sokujo* suggests "fast-brew"; the term is almost never seen on the bottle, however, as *sokujo-moto* has become the default brewing method, used in over 99 percent of all sake in existence.

To review: *yamahai* and *kimoto* are older, traditional methods that both utilize natural lactic bacteria to produce lactic acid, which then cleans out the environment in preparation for the sake yeast cells. *Sokujo-moto* gets lactic acid from the chemistry lab and adds it straightaway.

Note, *yamahai* and *kimoto* do *not* imply naturally occurring yeast; they imply naturally occurring lactic bacteria. Beware this misperception! Very, very rarely is naturally occurring yeast used. Just a handful of brewers take that risk. But when they do make sake that way, it absolutely must be either *kimoto* or *yamahai*, or it simply will not work.

There are real and perceived advantages to these methods. It takes about two weeks for the *yamahai* and *kimoto* methods to do their chemical thing before the yeast can be added. But *sokujo* cuts those two weeks out, shortening the production time significantly. The flavor of *sokujo* is also generally lighter and simpler, which appeals to (or has been made to appeal to, depending on whom you talk to) consumers.

The additional two weeks in *yamahai* and *kimoto* brewing means a total of one month just to create the yeast starter. But these two methods produce sake with more richness, umami, and depth. They can also be tarter, sweeter, and gamier.

Suehiro Yamahai Junmai

SUEHIRO SHUZO KK, FUKUSHIMA

Brown sugar and gamey-tart aromas. Soft feel, slightly sweet and earthy, lots of gamey depth. Very balanced yamahai.

When *yamahai* was first developed in 1909, Professor Kinichiro Kagi, before he could encourage the industry to begin to use this new method, had to get the kinks out. And so he practiced, further developing the method here at the Suehiro brewery. The *toji* that took over next did not like the process and stopped using it, but Suehiro revived it with delicious results a decade or so ago.

There are technical reasons a *toji* (brewer) may use one of these two methods. *Yamahai* tends to be more intense than *kimoto*, often showing more sweetness and gaminess as opposed to the subtle tartness and fine-grained quality to the flavor of many *kimoto*. Both *yamahai* and *kimoto* share some of the rich, umami-laden aspects when collectively compared to *sokujo*.

Yamahai in particular and *kimoto* to a degree are not always so wild and gamey. There are some that are powerfully so, with sweetness and acidity that may balance each other well but are nonetheless intense. However, there are many *yamahai* and *kimoto* that are barely noticeably gamey. Do not do yourself the disservice of assuming that a sake with *yamahai* or *kimoto* printed on the label is going to be a whack on your palate. It may be subtly richer, or not even noticeably different. In fact, some brewers avoid writing *yamahai* on the label for fear of inviting misperceptions from consumers. While sake made by one of these two methods tend to be wilder, there is in truth a range of flavors and styles to *yamahai* and *kimoto*. Just avoid prejudice!

These methods have nothing to do with the various grades of sake. Anything from a *futsu-shu* to a *daiginjo* can be a *yamahai*, *kimoto*, or *sokujo*. *Yamahai* richness may contradict the lightness of *daiginjo*, for example, but that combination does indeed exist, even if regular *junmai yamahai* are more common.

So the take-home here is that *yamahai* and *kimoto* share the use of natural lactic bacteria (*not* naturally occurring yeast!), take two weeks longer to make, and often taste wilder and more intense. *Yamahai* eschews the pole-mixing used in the original method of *kimoto* and is usually the gamier of the two. *Sokujo* is simpler and cleaner, albeit with less umami, and is completed in half the time.

No one style is better than another. Not until, that is, you find your own preferences.

Sake Yeast

Without yeast, there would be no sake. Nor would there be alcoholic beverages of any kind, or any bread for that matter.

Enzymes in the *koji* convert the starch in the rice to sugar. Yeast cells take in these sugar molecules and give off alcohol and carbon dioxide. But this process yields a host of other by-products as well, including various acids, amino acids, and other compounds, among them volatile acids and esters like ethyl caproate, isoamyl acetate, and ethyl acetate. Each of these leads to aromas with which we are much more familiar, such as apple, banana, and nail polish remover, respectively. Each yeast strain produces different compounds in different amounts.

What is worth remembering here is that more than anything else, yeast contributes to aromas in sake. Other factors—the kind of rice, how much it was milled, and how the *koji* was made—also contribute to aroma, and yeast affects other aspects of sake in addition to aroma. But when push comes to shove, what you smell in your sake is largely the result of the particular yeast strain used by the brewer.

There are other differences between yeast strains, and good reasons that a brewer might choose one strain over another. Some yeasts ferment more robustly and vigorously, while others are more lackadaisical. Some work better at warmer temperatures while others can tolerate colder ranges. One yeast type might peter out when the alcohol level of the *moromi* (fermenting mash) reaches 16 percent, while another might still crank it out at 20 percent.

And, importantly, some yeasts spew out significant amounts of acid, while others create just enough to make the sake pleasantly alive.

Like all living things, yeasts are also a product of their environment. If they are fed properly—not too much, not too little, and at just the right time—they will thrive. And even for any one yeast strain, just which esters, alcohols, and other compounds are produced is highly dependent on the temperature at which fermentation proceeds.

Until about a century ago, all sake yeast occurred naturally. It hovered in the air and clung to the rafters in a *kura*, and fell down into the inviting environment of the yeast starter (*moto*). The success of a brewery often depended on its resident strains of yeast.

In 1898, researchers isolated one basic strain of yeast in sake, and then another, and then another. These became available for brewers to buy, ensuring a source of pure yeast to brewers everywhere. Such yeasts are now distributed by an organization called Nihon Jozo Kyokai, known in English as the Brewing Society of Japan. The yeasts they sell to brewers in glass ampules are known, uninterestingly enough, simply by numbers like No. 7, No. 9, and No. 10. Each has its own characteristics, like strong fermentation or melon-like aromas, and brewers can pick and choose. Currently, the numbered yeasts run up to number 18, although the first few are no longer widely available, and a few more are outside of the standard numbering system. The most common yeasts are Nos. 7, 9, 10, 14, and 18, with aromatics *generally* increasing with the higher numbers.

However, as is often the case in the sake world, things are not quite that simple. While each of these yeasts is distributed by the Brewing Society of Japan, each has an original source too. For example, yeast No. 9 was first discovered at a brewery in Kumamoto making a sake called Koro. Each year, this brewery carefully isolates the yeast anew and sends it to the Society, where it is reproduced and distributed around Japan.

If a brewer is well connected, he can obtain the yeast from the original source in Kumamoto. Some say it is exactly the same; others say not. But the nomenclature of the yeast will differ, and after a while the number of names and variants starts to get a bit hairy. So, a No. 9 yeast is a No. 9 yeast—unless it isn't.

Also, several of the most common yeasts have a variant known as *awa nashi kobo* (non-foaming or foamless yeast). These are versions of the normal yeasts that do an almost identical job without producing the massive amounts of foam that rise and fall majestically throughout the course of fermentation.

Foamless yeasts can be desirable for a number of reasons. First is yields. A brewer can fit much more fermenting mash in a tank if he

Tamagawa "Jewel Dragon" Yamahai Junmai Daiginjo

KINOSHITA SHUZO KK, KYOTO

More subtly restrained than a yamahai made with naturally occurring yeast would lead one to believe. Chock full of umami, full yet layered and deep.

There are so many great yeast strains available that lead to predictable flavors and aromas that very few sake these days are made using spontaneous fermentation via yeast in the ambient environment. To go so far as to make a *daiginjo* that way calls for courage. British-born Nanbu *toji* Philip Harper pushes the envelope of sake-brewing traditional skill in this product, which instantly became a raging success.

does not need to leave room for the foam to rise and fall. Another is sanitation, since after the foam crescendos and then collapses it leaves a residue on the walls of the tank that, if not assiduously cleaned, can be a hotbed for bad bacteria.

The downside here is that brewers do not benefit from the information gained from looking at the appearance of the foam each day. And some brewers insist that the foamless variants are not as good, or at least, not exactly the same.

Foamless yeasts are designated by adding a –01 to the name. So No. 701 is a foamless version of No. 7, No. 901 is a foamless version of No. 9, and No. 1001 is a foamless version of No. 10. Naturally, No. 1801, the most recent addition to the family, is foamless, but interestingly there is not a foaming No. 18 on the market.

Original-source *kura* and the Brewing Society of Japan are not the only places to obtain yeast. Prefectural research centers are another. Brewers will often have their own proprietary yeast strains as well. Tokyo Agricultural University has developed a line of yeast for sake taken from flowers. In fact, there are countless strains of yeast out there, much to the consternation of the sake geeks who want to study the subject; there are simply too many yeasts to get one's head, or nose, around.

With so many good yeast strains on the market, why would anyone develop more? Product differentiation through aroma is one reason. Another reason is to win contests, in particular the national tasting of new sake each spring, called the Zenkoku Shinshu Kanpyokai (see page 110). If not overdone (a delicate balance to try and strike!), aroma can mean the difference between a medal and an also-ran sake.

New yeasts are always being introduced. Some will stand the test of time, and some will fall by the wayside for technical or marketing reasons. Yeast-related R&D efforts are certainly to be encouraged and admired, but this all just gets a bit hard to follow after a while.

The confusion is compounded by the fact that many brewers blend yeasts for higher grades of sake. A brewer may like the aromas one yeast provides, but since it is weak on body he blends it with another yeast that contributes needed fullness to the flavor, as one example. Furthermore, when brewers do blend yeasts, their methods vary significantly. Some use two yeasts in the same *moto*, some make two *moto* separately and then mix those, and others brew two separate batches of sake and blend the final product. Frustratingly to us laymen, the brewers' methods are all over the map.

And just to keep things interesting, a handful of brewers—only a very few—do not add yeast at all but allow the yeast that live in the *kura* (known as *yanetsuki-kobo*, or "yeast clinging to the rafters") to do its thing, just as it did in the days of old. The yeast that predominates here will naturally be very similar to what the brewers are using most of the time, since the microorganisms billow off the fermenting tanks and populate the air, walls, and rafters. But this method has its unpredictable side and does not allow the brewer to manage the process as precisely as he might prefer, so it is not commonly seen.

Note that if naturally occurring yeast is used, the method of creating the yeast starter must be either *yamahai* or *kimoto* (see page 76), as only those two traditional methods use the natural flow of chemistry that miraculously supports the development of pure sake yeast.

Finally, what is fascinating is how things vary greatly from *kura* to *kura*. How any individual yeast behaves in one location is very much tied in to the *kura* itself. Just how the wind blows, or what the typical ambient temperature is, or how the *kura* is set up and a plethora of other intangible factors make each place different. Some *kura* do well with a yeast that just does not work nearly as well elsewhere. Blending methods, too, can work well in one *kura* but not in another. And even the very nature of the brewery building has its say in the end.

The good news, however, is that all this need not concern us too much. Yes, yeasts can be hard to understand. But in the end, what we really need to bear in mind is that the choice of yeast has much to say about the aromas in sake.

The Connection Between Rice and Flavor

Since rice is the basic raw material of sake, it is tempting to look at sake rice as one might look at grapes in making wine—as the major determinant in flavor. Can this be done? Can we look at the strain of rice used and predict how the sake will taste? To some degree, yes. But the connection between the choice of rice and the characteristics of the final sake is not nearly as tight as the connection between the choice of grape and the nature of the resulting wine.

There are thousands of strains of rice in the world today, and hundreds in Japan alone. Currently, there are about one hundred that are designated as sake rice. New strains are created and old ones fall by the wayside each year, but the number continues to hover around one hundred. For most people who enjoy learning about sake, there are about a dozen strains of rice to remember. Particular flavors and tendencies are roughly associated with them, but depending on how the sake was brewed, these flavors will be less noticeable in some sake than in others.

While any good wine professional can fairly often taste a wine and identify the grape, it's not that easy to do with sake. It's not impossible, and it can be done by some people and in certain situations, but the connection between the rice used and the final flavor in sake is not that clear cut. This is because, due to the extensive manhandling of the raw materials that go into a sake, two brewers can take the same rice and make totally different, seemingly unrelated sake.

Consider the milling. A sake made with rice milled down to a *seimai-buai* of only 70 percent will be very different from one made using the same rice milled down to 35 percent. And even for two sake made with the same rice at the same *seimai-buai*, the way the *koji* is made can make one sweet and the other dry, or anything in between. The yeast used, the nature of the water, the fermentation temperature, and the post-brewing processing steps such as pasteurization, dilution, storage, and temperature control, and much more will also guide a sake down one of many different paths.

While these other factors are important to the final product, the various major rice types do have identifiable flavors and describable threads of consistency running through them. Learning to identify these is a matter of exposure and experience. I recall being on a tasting panel assessing about a hundred sake made with Yamada Nishiki rice and another hundred made from Omachi rice. The event was put on by the agricultural cooperative of Okayama Prefecture, which grows lots of both types of rice. Running through a hundred of one type of rice and then moving on to a hundred of another is like moving into a different universe; they can seem like totally different beverages. While we rarely have the chance to see a hundred manifestations of two different rice types lined up like that, if one is exposed to such a situation, the differences become very clear indeed.

The challenge arises because, although a rice type will have a typical set of associated flavors, the rice is not always used in such a way as to enhance them. There are several reasons why a brewery will choose a rice that go beyond its typical resulting flavors. Characteristics like how it behaves during fermentation, how easy it is to use, how predictably it dissolves, its price, and its availability are all part of the decision. The aimed-for flavor is just one part of the rationale.

Is it possible to identify the sake rice used in blind tasting? To a degree. If you put a half dozen sake in front of someone with significant tasting experience and announce that one of them is, for example, made with Yamada Nishiki and is *a typical manifestation* of that rice, then yes, it can be identified. If you had four or five of the major rice types and each was, again, a good representative of those four or five, most decent tasters would nail them, or at least come close. However, it might be more challenging for those with less exposure and experience with sake than it would be for someone with the same amount of experience in wine to identify the grape.

Shichida Junmai

TENZAN SHUZO KK, SAGA

Butter-honey aromas evolve into a flavor defined first by a mouth-filling umami yet is overall slightly dry and astringent at the end. The flavor seems to evolve with each sip.

The main brand at this *kura* is Tenzan. The Shichida brand was created a few years back and is reserved for sake made with locally grown Yamada Nishiki rice. It is a great example of how locally grown rice can impart a unique connection to the region, as the local climate is good for growing that rice, and the brewing style of the brewer lends itself well to bringing out its best aspects.

For most folks, most of the time, it would likely be difficult. But that's fine, as there is no need at all to work that hard. More than the choice of rice, how the overall package appeals to us is by far most important.

Let's look at some of the major rice types and how they might be typically described.

Yamada Nishiki is the most widely used sake rice. It is prized for how easy it is to use. Because it is so popular, there are reams of data on it, and any brewing problem is likely to have been faced before, so it is solvable with a phone call. Yamada Nishiki leads to full, billowing flavors that are often a bit sweet and rich yet smooth. The second most widely used rice, Gohyakumangoku, is a mouthful to say but on the contrary leads to light and airy sake. Omachi rice is quite tight and almost astringent and herbal, as is Hattan Nishiki. Miyama Nishiki yields light and narrow-flavored sake, often with (to me) a milky richness to it.

These are just a few examples of what the top five rice types typically taste like. Not all sake rice is as easily described. Most are not, if only because they are used much less frequently than these five, meaning there are significantly fewer products from which to garner such descriptions.

While not as tight as grapes-to-wine, yes, the rice-to-sake flavor connection is there. It is surely worth your effort to try to notice the basic characteristics of the main types. The more you taste, the easier it gets.

Regionality

Japan is a bit smaller than California and runs about eight hundred miles roughly northeast to southwest. Today sake is made in every single one of its forty-seven prefectures. (A couple prefectures just make a token amount and did not make any sake at all until recently.)

Each prefecture has its own terrain and climate. But does sake, like much wine, have regionality? That is, does sake from one part of Japan have a style or profile that can be associated with it, and sake from another region a different but just as identifiable nature?

The short answer is yes, it does, and regionality in sake is extremely interesting to study. However, it is decidedly vaguer and not as clearly delineated or identifiable as it is in the wine world. Some prefectures reflect regional distinctions and some do not have much individuality at all. This does not mean that the sake from those nondescript regions are not good. On the contrary, sake from some regions not known for their sake can be outstanding. But overall, perhaps 60 percent of the regions of Japan have at least some style of sake associated with them.

So yes, sake has regionality.

Furthermore, in any region that does have an associated regional style, not all the *kura* in the region conform to that style. You'll always have dissenters, deliberately or otherwise. But in any given region that has a style, perhaps 60 to 70 percent of the *kura* in that area will brew sake in that identifiable style. Again, that is enough for a passing grade.

A number of factors have contributed to the sake style of each region. First there is climate. The temperature of a region affects the flavors of sake immensely. The northern regions of Japan are of course much colder than those in the south. Sake made in the northeast part of Japan is both fermented and subsequently matured at lower temperatures than sake made in the southwest part of Japan. Colder fermentation and storage temperatures generally lead to lighter, cleaner sake. Warmer temperatures lead to fuller, broader flavors. Neither is intrinsically better than the other; it is simply a matter of preference.

Another factor that affects the style of sake from a given region is cuisine. Long ago when regional styles came into being, people in the mountains did not have a daily diet of fresh sashimi. Most of what they had in those cold, damp regions was preserved food, often heavy, sweet, and salty. Naturally enough, the sake that developed around food like that was sweeter and heavier, so as to complement it.

Contrast this with towns near big fishing ports, where long ago even the peasants were enjoying fresh fish as often as they could catch it. The sake brewed near these places was much lighter and softer due in part to what the people there ate.

The rice that grew in each part of Japan also contributed to sake styles, at least before rice could be practically shipped to here and there. The rice that grows in the west is larger than that which grows up north, and along with the warmer temperatures, this leads to bigger flavors than its cold-weather, smaller-grain counterparts. Water plays its part too, although its role is more tenuous because water is not necessarily consistent across any given region. Water may affect the style of sake in any one given brewery, but with a few notable exceptions it is hard to link region and water.

One more factor that traditionally

affected sake styles is the guilds of *toji* (brewers) that were dominant in each region. These guys (and guys they were, back in the day) would farm their own land in the summer and travel to nearby breweries in the fall for the upcoming brewing season. Come spring, the *toji* would return home, and between farming chores they would drink together and exchange notes. Eventually they created structured organizations to aid, assist, and promote their brewing prowess. What this means is that the various guilds all had their own methods and tricks of the trade. Most of these were born of experience gained in local breweries, using local rice in local climates.

The various guilds then developed methods that led to noticeable characteristics in their final sake. "Their sake is a true Nanbu guild style," or "That guy is not really brewing in a true Tanba Toji manner"—these kinds of

Tensei "Song of the Sea" Junmai Ginjo

KUMAZAWA SHUZO KK, KANAGAWA

Bold melon and banana aromas, and vivid flavors reminiscent of those aromas. Balanced intensity.

Kanagawa Prefecture is anything but a bastion of sake production. Situated just south of Tokyo, there are less than fifteen *kura* here, none of them very large or famous. Tensei is one example of how fine sake can be found even in regions not known for it. The rice and yeast are from far, far away. But the skilled young *toji* is local, and the company is tied to the region in many ways, including the name Tensei (referring to the climate of the region) and involvement with the community.

comments can still be heard muttered by those who are deep enough into it (and overheard by people like me who just happen to be standing near them).

Ironically, some of these same factors that have contributed to regionality in sake are today also partly responsible for the undoing of regional distinctions.

Consider cuisine. These days, people in the mountains far from the sea can enjoy fresh sashimi on a daily basis with a bicycle ride to the local convenience store. And the fresh-fish folks down by the ocean might prefer steak some nights. As availability of certain foods blossoms and local cuisine loses its grip, the need for a particular local style of sake changes as well.

Another break from custom is a change in the traditional *toji* system. Long ago, a *kura* would almost certainly employ a *toji* from the closest guild, but today a *toji* can come from just about anywhere. A *kura* might even brew by themselves, without a *toji* from any guild. Brewing technologies and methods are more widely accessible now, so a brewery may employ methods or styles that are different from what would lead to the erstwhile local style of sake.

Nor are there any laws to keep regional styles in place or to dictate what raw materials or methods can be used. Brewers are free to make sake any way they please. The rice used in a local brew can come from anywhere in Japan. Most *kura* try to use at least some local rice, and a few make a big deal of using *only* local rice (good on them!). But many insist upon Yamada Nishiki from Hyogo for their top *daiginjo*, and as good as this is for the sake itself, using rice from far away for your local sake is a chink in the armor of regionality.

Furthermore, within any one prefecture that does in fact have a clear style, inevitably a handful of *kura* will not be consistent with that style. They may have had other influences, like one particular *toji* or a former owner who had his own ideas of how sake should taste. Or perhaps they just want to differentiate themselves from the pack. But there will always be some that make sake that is different from the local norm.

Modern market conditions are another reality with which brewers must contend. The amazing infrastructure that, today, lets me get any sake I want from any part of the country delivered to my door the next day means brewers now make sake for markets much bigger than just the local yokels. As such they need to make sake that appeals to people in the big cities, if not all over the world. Even if such sake is undoubtedly tasty, it does become homogenized in terms of style. The *ginjo* of a given region tends to taste like the *ginjo* of all regions, rather than the original style of sake from that area. With many smaller brewers seeing their market for *futsu-shu* dry up as they lose it to larger companies with better economies of scale, more production goes toward such homogenized *ginjo* and premium sake. This is not a bad thing—but it often means a shift from original regional styles.

Having contributing and detracting factors all in play at the same time leads to a very vague but interesting state of affairs. There is, however, a general but useful rule that can be applied to sake regionality, one that stands up to scrutiny and is echoed by experts in the industry (meaning: I didn't just make this up!).

The farther northeast you go, the more fine-grained and compact the sake gets. It is often light, delicate, and dry, but not always. It is commonly tight, as if a lot of flavor got compacted into a narrow girth. And conversely, the farther west you go, the more big-boned, rich, and broad the sake flavors get; more sake in this part of Japan are heavier and sweet.

This is due to everything presented above: climate, rice, *toji* guilds, and more. And while this is admittedly a big generalization, it's a workable one.

Along this northeast–southwest continuum of fine-grained to big-boned sake, there are exceptions. Plenty of 'em. There are entire prefectures that are doing their own thing stylewise, and others that have no clear style, great stuff though their sake may be. Still, this rule applies more than half the time, which means we can use it as a reference.

There are a handful of easily remembered examples of regions with a clear style. Niigata is easily the place with the most identifiable style: dry, light, and pristine. *Tanrei-karakuchi* is the term they have adopted, and an extremely high percentage of the almost one hundred breweries in the prefecture fit this description well. Next would likely be the Nada region in Hyogo Prefecture, the largest brewing region in the country, which has dry, rich sake that is decidedly not ostentatious. Comparatively close by is the Fushimi region of Kyoto, whose soft water leads to gentle, delicate, and somewhat sweet sake that goes decidedly well with the refined cuisine of Kyoto.

Hiroshima, or most of it anyway, has soft water that contributes to soft and sweet sake, whereas Kochi on the island of Shikoku has extremely dry sake with a solid structure that is a result of its culture of drinking significantly more per capita than the average region. Yamagata makes a higher ratio of *ginjo* than any other prefecture, so much of the sake from there is light and fruity.

Fukushima is blessed with ocean coast, plains, and mountains, giving it a wider range of sake types than most places and making it hard to assign an overall style to sake from that prefecture. It deserves special mention because it is one of several prefectures affected by the massive earthquake and nuclear accident that occurred on March 11, 2011. By that time the sake-brewing season was wrapping up, and there was no rice in the ground. Only a couple of *kura* were so close to the nuclear reactor that they had to evacuate the area. All the other breweries in the region were far enough away and protected with thick-walled, sealed buildings that kept the sake safe.

The Fukushima sake industry has responded to public concern in effective and convincing ways. Every aspect and ingredient is checked several times. The rice that goes into the sake, the water used in brewing, and the final product are all tested by a third party. Every single bottle of sake from Fukushima is tested and not a single drop has been found to have a higher-then-permissible level of cesium or other adverse elements.

★ ★ ★

The regional styles discussed here are but a few examples, and because this whole subject is a bit vague and open to interpretation there will certainly be various opinions as to how all the regions compare.

To me one of the most enjoyable aspects of sake is getting at least a basic grip on sake regionality and then comparing the taste of each sake to what I think I know about its region. This can be a bit of a hit or miss exercise, but it is is nevertheless always an interesting one.

HOW THE INDUSTRY REALLY WORKS

The Sake Industry

Like any industry—and in particular like any traditional industry—the sake world has its quirks. And like most quirks, they may not be apparent at first. But some of them are restraining the industry's growth and potential. And three in particular are doing the most damage:

1. The sake industry is incredibly polarized.
2. The sake industry reflects an inherent economic paradox.
3. The sake industry is, for most participants, simply not very profitable.

Let's consider these three in more detail.

The sake world is incredibly polarized.

Currently, there are about 1,250 sake breweries in operation (as of spring 2014). Among those, perhaps 17 breweries are massive, and about 1,000 are tiny. The remaining 200 or so breweries are somewhere in the middle. Those 15 massive breweries comprise only 1.4 percent of the total but make about 55 percent of the sake produced every year and accordingly pay about half of the alcohol tax that the government collects. Conversely, more than 60 percent of all the *kura* are tiny and combine for a scant 5 percent of the taxes. Now that's polarized!

It is important to stress that neither extreme is better than the other. Some folks like to disdain the large companies (although it used to be the other way around). That is certainly not fair and comes from a misinformed mindset. The breweries at both ends of the spectrum are staffed with great people, and both large and tiny breweries make some great sake—as well as some mediocre sake. Certainly there are well-run and less-well-run companies, but size or scale of operations is not what separates these.

Both ends of the spectrum have their strengths and their weaknesses. Large companies are viewed as being stable, reliable, and consistent, as well as offering outstanding value for the price of their products, which their scale of operations makes possible. Smaller brewers sometimes have more character and more romantic stories in their backgrounds. Most of what the national brands ("NB") make is inexpensive, lower-grade sake, at least in terms of sheer volume of production. Because this is their most visible type of product it can adversely and unfairly affect their reputation. But a scant few decades ago, it was the smaller brewers, or *jizake* producers, who were often

Kenbishi Mizuho Junmai
KENBISHI SHUZO KK, HYOGO

Earthy brown sugar-laced aroma, typical of good mature sake. The rich maturity continues in the deep, refined flavor, which is dried out by a proper acidity.

Kenbishi is one of the most historically significant sake breweries in the industry, and one of the overall most interesting. It has basically thrived on its reputation for over 500 years! Lately, the owners are modernizing their approach to marketing, but they maintain older, traditional methods of brewing. They do a lot of blending here, and this particular product is a blend of several years of sake, with the average being three years old.

considered hit-or-miss, lacking the reputation of the NB companies. While collective reputations have changed and perhaps equalized a bit, a wide chasm between these two extremes still exists.

Naturally, the objectives and priorities of the few large companies are totally different from those of the many small companies. What they want to accomplish—the type of sake they want to make and the market segments they target—are different. With such diverse objectives, the ways in which the brewers want to spend money on marketing are vastly different as well.

This means that there is very little industry-wide cooperation on the all-important marketing front. Note, the big breweries and small breweries don't hate each other. It's not as if they're at each other's throats. Sure, a bit of bad-mouthing takes place here and there, nothing excessive. But in an industry that has been in a gentle but steady decline for decades, what needs to happen is across-the-board cooperation so that everyone benefits, and that is not happening.

To a certain degree, this is understandable. If almost all of a company's products are inexpensive sake, the company will not want to put its efforts into marketing premium sake. Conversely, if all a brewer makes is *ginjo* (as is the case for a handful of producers), they will want to make the most of that fact in their marketing communications. Both large and small companies are fully functioning entities that pay salaries every month, feed families, and form objectives with clear strategies. How they market their products—or do not market them—is in tune with these objectives. So, although the sake industry needs cooperation throughout, it is not likely to happen any time soon—at least not on a large scale.

I recall visiting one of the top twenty breweries a few years ago, and after a meeting in which the various marketing and production department heads presented their overviews to me, the young president asked me bluntly, "John, what is it that you would like to ask of the industry?"

"I'd like you all to cooperate more," I responded immediately. I did not even need to think about it.

He flashed a cynical smile and said, "Aw, you had to start with the most difficult request, didn't you!"

Perhaps things will improve, if only out of necessity rather than spontaneous goodwill. But the industry as a whole could certainly benefit from more cooperation.

The sake industry reflects an inherent economic paradox.

Another important aspect of the structure of the sake world is that almost all—90 percent—of the companies are family-owned businesses. Perhaps fifty or so belong to one of three or four umbrella companies owning a handful of breweries, and a few others are owned by other parent companies. Aside from these exceptions, almost all *sakagura* have been handed down in a family from generation to generation.

This is significant for two reasons. One is that breweries are limited in their capital. The other is that the priorities of the directors might not be what you expect.

Family businesses, even large and well-run operations, generally do not have access to the same capital as publicly traded companies. This limits their growth in many ways, not the least of which is how well they engage in marketing operations. Large family-owned sake companies do have larger pools of available capital, but they are still small compared to public companies.

Why would they not, then, open up to outside investment that is needed to grow and flourish, helping themselves and, by extension,

the industry? Because sometimes the significance and pressure of being responsible for a
family business that has lasted for many generations leads to risk aversion.

The one thing many *kuramoto* do not
want to do is to give away the family business
in the name of growth; many would rather go
under. It's not that they do not want to grow.
Surely they do; every business wants to flourish. Rather, they have other priorities, or more
dominating figures of merit, that are inherent in
their nature as family-owned businesses. Often,
there is significant pressure to pass the business
on to the next generation—at which point the
head of the company is off the hook. This is
not true of all sake brewers, but it applies often
enough.

So we have an industry that reflects an
economic paradox in which collectively, the
goal of all members is to grow and flourish, but
some of those members have priorities that do
not align with that goal. And this is not likely
to change.

The sake industry is, for most participants, simply not very profitable.

Finally, brewing and selling sake is simply not a
very profitable business—at least not any more,
not for most of its members. Surveys in recent
years have revealed that only about 40 to 45
percent of all sake producers are reasonably
profitable; more than half the industry is in the
red or minimally profitable.

There are numerous reasons for this. For
one, rice is just darn expensive, at least in Japan.
Sake rice is even pricier. Making good sake is
an expensive process as well. Everything from
labor to energy to marketing costs a lot of
money. Gone are the days when a *sakagura* was
the only game in town and marketing and shipping were not significant costs.

Another reason is that sake prices are often
based on the cost of the cheapest sake, and

these are priced based on price wars. This leads to a lot of downward pressure on prices, significantly limiting profitability.

It is important to remember that many companies that brew sake have other "side" businesses that are often much more profitable than the "main" business of brewing. The company may own a lot of land and draw from that. Or it may run a totally unrelated, quite profitable business for which the sake-brewing arm of the family conglomerate is just a calling card. Although not all *kura* are on the verge of disappearing, sake brewing is often not a profitable endeavor.

★ ★ ★

The sake industry is a great industry, filled with wonderful and extremely interesting people. Its idiosyncrasies are functions of both what it makes (a craft beverage) and who makes it (families, not corporations). It is polarized, paradoxical, and challenging.

How can we help? What are we to do? *Drink lots of sake!* Improved sake consumption will make most of the problems go away. Other issues will move toward resolution and compromise, step by step. Some issues will never go away, but perhaps their resolution is not all that necessary. These interesting quirks are all part and parcel of an ancient and traditional industry.

Sake Pricing

Sake is fairly priced 90 percent of the time. This is perhaps one of my favorite things to say to make sake more approachable. I am sure there are other opinions, but I stand by this one.

If we were to walk down a long row of sake bottles at a retail shop, we would stop at each one, and for nine out of ten bottles we would say with a shrug, "Yeah; that's about right." Perhaps one bottle in each group would get a wince, and we might say, "Nah, that's over-priced," or "Now *this* one is a deal, actually!"

How are sake prices really set? What affects prices? What makes one sake more or less expensive than the one next to it? There are a handful of factors.

First there are the obvious things, like the cost of the raw materials. Rice—especially sake rice—is expensive. It is perhaps the biggest factor that drives price. Not only do brewers start with expensive rice, but to make top-grade sake, they then mill the bejeezus out of it, and end up using half or less of it.

In fact, the fastest way for a brewer to lower market price is to use less expensive rice. This is why we sometimes see *koji* being made with very good rice that is milled to a high degree, and the remaining 80 percent or so of the rice used being a less expensive variety, or milled less. *Koji* represents 20 percent of the rice but applies 80 percent of the leverage in terms of the nature of the final product.

Next is the labor intensive nature of sake making. Soaking the rice by hand, making *koji* carefully by hand, fermenting for a long time in a tank, and drip pressing—these are all things that drive up the cost of sake. When making premium sake, especially when compared to inexpensive sake, a brewer will never ferment to get the maximum amount of alcohol, nor will the brewer try to squeeze every last drop out of the mash when fermentation is complete. Both of these things would yield more sake, but at the cost of smoothness and balance in the flavor. These processes all limit yields, and thereby drive up price.

The size of a brewery is another price driver. Bigger breweries can do everything just as well but more cheaply than smaller outfits, so the prices of sake across the grades are usually slightly cheaper for the larger breweries. Expressed conversely, the lack of an economy of scale drives prices up for the smaller brewers that make up almost the entire industry.

What all this means is that it is hard to find

Born Gold Junmai Daiginjo

KATO KICHIBEE SHOUTEN, FUKUI

More herbal and floral than overtly fruity, the aromas are still quite pronounced. The flavors are bright and vivid and include crisp apple and rice, yet are rounded at the corners due to the low-temperature maturation.

This brewery produces a wide range of products, some of them pricey. But this *junmai daiginjo* is a great value considering the quality behind it—rarely are *junmai daiginjo* available in this price range. Certainly no corners were cut, as it has been aged a full year at −10°C before bottling and shipping.

premium sake at rock-bottom prices. There is a lot of really decent wine for very reasonable prices in the world today. However, sake has trouble competing in that realm (the under-twenty-US-dollars-a-bottle market) as it is simply much more difficult to field decent sake at low prices.

Although sake has various pressures keeping prices up, it also has pressures keeping prices low. While this sounds great to us consumers, it does not allow breweries to make a decent profit on their high-end products. The situation is also not comparable to the wine industry, which has a large sector of product at extremely high prices of which consumers simply cannot get enough.

What keeps sake prices low? Spec-hunters, peer pressure, and trickle-up effects.

Spec-hunters are buyers who buy on spec. They will, for example, refuse to pay a certain amount of money for a product unless it has a certain *seimai-buai*. While they are free of course to haggle and maintain their own expectations of value, this creates a problem: the true quality of a sake is not found in the number that expresses the *seimai-buai*!

A restaurant or retail buyer might tell a brewer, "That product has a *seimbai-buai* of 60 percent; I will only pay *this* much for it." To which the brewer would mentally respond, "Hey, buddy, have you *tasted* it yet?" But saying so would not get him far, and so the price is forced down.

Another brewer, when asked how he sets his prices, flashed a wry smile and replied that for each of his premium products, he would like to charge a bit more. "But there's a kind of peer pressure at work. The guy down the street and other brewers in my area are only charging so much for a comparable product. So I cannot charge more even if I wanted to."

Complicating this is that there are some brewers—not all, but some—that run other businesses that are very profitable. The *sakagura* part of the family business might have been operating centuries longer than the side business, so many brewers do not want to give it up—and surely many of them love brewing sake. But it means that these companies do not actually have to be profitable making sake; the side business takes care of that. So they charge less than they need to, which can potentially limit what others charge.

Then there is the trickle-up effect. Very often sake prices are restrained by what the least expensive sake costs. If bottom-shelf *futsu-shu* costs a certain price, then the *futsu-shu* one level up (there are several levels, although they are not official grades) should be a few percentage points higher. So there seems to be this underlying thinking that when one kind of sake is priced at a certain level, the standard pricing for each ascending grade has a natural limit based on that of each grade preceding it.

Again, this is not necessarily a bad way to look at it. However, bear in mind that almost all the *futsu-shu* out there is made by the largest breweries with the best economies of scale and that they are fighting price wars in the trenches for this kind of sake. The point is, those prices are kept artificially low, and they then trickle up and restrain prices across the entire range of sake product levels. This in turn affects profitability and thereby the health of the industry.

Sake, in effect, is getting squeezed from both ends. Prices cannot get too low or too high. So, good yet inexpensive sake is rarer than good yet inexpensive wine; but also, high-end sake is not nearly as expensive as high-end wine. Sake prices exist in a fairly narrow bandwidth.

There are of course a number of things that potentially affect wine prices to which sake is immune. For example, there is no such thing as a vintage system in sake. Surely there are good years and less good years, but as sake is not aged, and because brewers try to minimize differences and strive for consistency, vintage is not a factor.

There are also no publications or individuals assessing sake and assigning products influential numerical scores, at least not in Japan. There are a couple breweries that can and do raise prices on reputation alone, so reputation can impact price.

But most factors that affect the price of sake, be they tangible or less so, are not entirely obvious.

The Annual Japan Sake Awards

A plethora of tasting contests exist these days. They seem to take place all the time, put on by one group or another, all with exemplary panels. While the main events seem focused on wine, many of them incorporate sake as well.

But these contests are all newcomers to the game when compared to Japan's Zenkoku Shinshu Kanpyokai, literally translated as "the National New Sake Tasting Competition."

The affair is pretty much just what it sounds like. Officially known in English as the Annual Japan Sake Awards, it is a national tasting competition for the just-brewed sake of the recently concluded brewing season. This historically and culturally significant event has been running since 1910 and was until recently sponsored by one ministry of the government or another. However, recent budget concerns have almost totally weaned the event off of government money, and it is now run by the industry. That may change again in the future.

The event is sponsored by the National Research Institute of Brewing (NRIB), who over the decades has done much research on yeast and other micro-organisms, as well as general sake-brewing practices that have made sake into the fine stuff it is. Unglamorously, however, the institute was founded to ensure that brewers could brew sake without screwing it up, as sake was in the early 20th century a significant portion of tax revenue for the government. The tasting competition came about as a way to give brewers a chance to show their stuff, polish their skills, and develop new techniques that would help the overall quality of sake. In this it has undoubtedly succeeded.

Every spring, brewers that want to participate (about three-fourths of the industry) submit several bottles of sake by a certain date. The entry will be *daiginjo*, and it will be intense. Rarely is it *junmai* since the brewers want to take advantage of the aroma enhancement produced by the technique of adding a bit of alcohol. The submitted sake will be very impactful and timed so that its very short peak will take place during the few days it is in the hands of the judging panels.

The judging method is brilliant in its simplicity. Up to forty judges taste blindly from identical tumblers, and a score of one to five is assigned. The judges know nothing about the sake at all. A score of one is great, three is mediocre, and five indicates something is off. That's it. No panels, pondering, or discussion. The scores from the judges are averaged, and a bell-curve-like line is used as a cut-off. Then the process is repeated. The second round is even harsher, with a one, two, or three being the only scores, again with one being best. The sake that score above that vaguely defined bell-curve demarcation after the second round win gold. Those that make it to the second round but do not make the final cut are awarded a prize that corresponds to silver.

Just where the cut-off is made in the two rounds is very Japanese in its beautiful vagueness. No particular numerical score is used as a cutoff to make it to the second round, nor is there a defined number of sake that make it there or that ultimately win gold. Rather, the judges look for a gap in the scores, a place to neatly make the cut that shows a fairly clear differential. This means the number of awards varies slightly from year to year.

While, incredibly, very few consumers

know or care about the contest or its results, it is a very important and prestigious competition for members of the industry. Winning a gold is an accomplishment, and going too long without winning one is a source of pressure, at least to some. To win with controlled regularity, year in and year out, is extremely difficult and is therefore highly respected.

The sake submitted to these contests is not, however, regular sake, the sake we buy in the store from those same producers. In most cases, it has been brewed especially for this contest. In truth, it is a bit too intense to enjoy very much of; it is rather like *daiginjo* on steroids. While fascinating, the flavor and aroma are especially strong. More than anything else, sake for this contest is brewed to exude an absolute minimum of flaws, and this is generally what you will find. It will conform to a very tight flavor profile with little deviation, be precisely

Eikun "Ichigin" Junmai Daiginjo
SAITO SHUZO KK, KYOTO

Melon, banana, and a citrus touch in a tightly bound aroma; soft, eminently refined, and deep flavor, ever so slightly on the sweet side.

Eikun holds the record for consecutive gold medals in the Zenkoku Shinshu Kampyokai competition, at fourteen in a row. Although tied with another brewer, all of Eikun's golds came from one *kura*. It is hard enough to win one gold; winning often is impressive. Winning most of the time is outstanding. Winning fourteen years in a row is simply astounding.

balanced, and have an absolute minimum of off-flavors and fragrances. But it is not something for relaxing with and sipping over a couple of hours with food.

You might ask, "What, then, is the point if we cannot buy it, and it does not resemble their everyday brew?"

The results are an indication of a brewer's skill in being able to conform to a very constricted profile, to exercise absolute control over the brewing process. This is where the true significance of this competition comes in: when a brewer sells great sake to consumers and also consummates that with regular golds, we can be sure they know what they are doing and can trust in the quality of their sake.

There have been other contests over the years as well, such as an autumn event for sake destined for the market. But all other competitions have fallen by the wayside or been eliminated entirely, and the Annual Japan Sake Awards is by far the most significant.

The event is not without its minor politics. Over the years, a handful of brewers have boycotted the contest, ostensibly on the grounds it meant little as it did not judge market sake. Some of those boycotting companies were large companies that presumably could not risk tarnishing their reputation by revealing that, despite their marketing, they were not that good. But today, almost all the large producers participate and do fairly well.

There are also small brewers that simply do not have the wherewithal or resources to brew sake especially for one contest. Some will sit it out, while others will just ship along a regular *daiginjo* and hope for the best.

Little twists in the rules take place from time to time. A while back the NRIB began separating the sake into two categories: one made with Yamada Nishiki rice and one made with anything else. They did this because no brewer dared to use any rice other than Yamada

Nishiki, which defeated the push-the-envelope goal of the contest. More recently, they felt they had accomplished their goal and eliminated this rule, so that all sake are now tasted together again, regardless of the rice used.

Some regions are more dominating than others. For example, almost every year, Niigata Prefecture takes more golds than anywhere else, although Nagano, Yamagata, Hiroshima, Fukushima, and Kyoto also do well.

The various *toji* guilds, prefectures, and tax regions also host sake competitions that are run in a similar way. These contests may vary in date and in their grades of sake, but they are judged fairly and blindly. Still, the Annual Japan Sake Awards remains "the big show."

In the end, breweries will have only submitted a small amount of their sake batch to the contest. The rest is often mixed in with other sake, usually *daiginjo*, and sold as such. But if you poke around, you can sometimes find sake from contest batches being sold on the market. It is quite interesting to taste and experience a somewhat toned-down version of what surely was a concentrated package of sake flavors and aromas.

Each year in June, the Japan Sake and Shochu Makers Association puts on an event for the public in Tokyo. At that gala event is a room in which all the contest sake are lined up for the public to taste. This is surely the best way to experience what contest sake is all about.

Rice Distribution

"It's complicated."

One of the more idiosyncratic aspects of the sake world is the distribution system through which brewers get their rice. It certainly is not simple, and at one time it probably made sense. Many do benefit from the system—both brewers and farmers—but it serves others less. And, of course, there are those who have the means and cleverness to work around it if needed. Let's look at it a bit more closely.

Realize first that sake brewers do not grow their own rice. Since just after World War II, business entities have not been permitted to grow rice in Japan. All rice instead is to be grown and sold by individual farmers. Things have changed a little recently and there are some exceptions, but basically sake brewers cannot own rice fields or grow their own rice.

Why is this the case? To prevent the reconsolidation of farmland. Long ago, owners of huge tracts of land wielded total control, rather than the peasants living and growing on the land. For reasons beyond my comprehension (although my sense of common decency says it's not cool), this was not a stable situation economically. Regardless of the reasoning, this keeps rice plots spread out and small, with the average plot being about 1.65 acres, compared to farms typically 160 times that in the U.S.

This led to the creation of agricultural cooperatives, about which more can be written than the scope of this book could hope to contain. In short, local farmers distribute their rice to the market through local agricultural co-ops, from whom they are often obligated to buy fertilizers, insecticides, and more. But these co-ops then negotiate prices and secure livelihoods for the local farmers and others. They are also necessarily competitive organizations, and they do their best to promote the brands of rice that grow best in their region.

For many brewers, this is the easiest way to go. They place an order for a certain type of rice grown in a certain region, and almost always, they will get it. They cannot specify just who the grower is, but they can specify the variety, inspected grade, and region. While sometimes shortages do occur, they almost always get what they ordered.

Then, a scant fifteen or so years ago, laws changed, allowing brewers to bypass the co-ops and form contracts with farmers to buy rice directly. This is great for a number of reasons. Brewers can "see the faces" of the rice

Chikurin Fukamari "Depth" Junmai

MARUMOTO SHUZO KK, OKAYAMA

Subtle and soft aromas and flavors, leaning more richly floral and earthy than fruity. The flavors are defined by the sake's overall softness and receptiveness to a wide range of food.

Much of the rice used at this brewery is grown by the company itself, which owns some of the rice fields near the brewery and rents many other fields from older farming families (who are happy to cooperate as it keeps the land arable). While they cannot supply all the rice the company requires, the rice for this particular product is grown entirely by the brewery workers.

producers, dictate a bit more about how it is grown, and observe the rice at every step of its evolution. However, there are also downsides to contracting with single producers.

For example, what if there is a bad year and the harvest is poor? When one buys from an agricultural co-op that draws from many growers, it is easy to cover those shortages. Sure, somebody somewhere gets stiffed, but it's a game of supply and demand and of who orders first.

And such harvest shortages can often be predicted, allowing all the brewers to make alternate plans and to work with the co-ops to secure the rice they need, thus spreading the pain fairly across the industry.

But if a brewer buys from one farmer drawing from just a few fields, a bad year means less rice, which must then be bought later, elsewhere, and may be neither the quality nor the price that was initially sought, and possibly not even the same variety!

What if there is a bumper crop? While that sounds great, it may not be. Again, buying from a co-op is no problem: "You ordered this much, you get this much. The surplus is our problem." But if you buy via contract on a field and the farmer has a bumper crop, you are stuck paying for and dealing with all the excess rice from that field. After all, the grower reserved it all for you. And while you might be tempted to think, "Well, just make more sake with it!" it is not that simple practically, economically, or even legally.

Of course, there are ways to work around both of these issues; the point here is simply to show the pros and cons of each, and how big an endeavor procuring rice is for sake brewers.

Only about 1.4 percent of all rice grown in Japan is sake rice. Obviously, it is not a cash crop, nor is it the priority for most farmers or co-ops. Wide plains are reserved for more lucrative-to-grow table rice, and often sake rice gets relegated to the harder-to-till parcels. Not always, but often.

Also, a few years back, it became legal for some business entities—including brewers—to grow rice. One would think, "Hey, now this changes everything!" But in reality, very few have begun to do that. Surely many welcome the idea in theory, but gearing up to farm when you do not have the people, experience, and tools is a major undertaking. In addition, the relationships with those who can already do it well are in place. The predominant attitude is to let it ride.

But in truth there are many patterns. One brewer I know maintains about twenty-five fields around his region, small parcels of land that are owned by folks too old to work them anymore. My brewer friend rents them for very little, and it is a win-win situation. He gets to grow his rice his way, and he keeps the land arable, which the owners like.

"It has its attendant issues," he lamented hesitatingly. "Often, those old folks can be a pain in the neck."

Why then, I suggested, do you not just buy the land from them? The terseness of the wave of his hand as he dismissed the suggestion clearly conveyed its ridiculousness.

"Land prices are high; profit margins on rice and sake are minuscule. It would take me well over a full century to reap a return on my investment!"

So while many brewers might like the romantic notion of growing their own sake rice, it is often not a practical option.

But the complications are not only about who can actually grow the rice. Rice distribution and supply—as well as the murky rules surrounding them—can also be significantly affected by government allocations of land and related subsidies. While this is a complicated issue, let's try to tackle it.

First, understand that while the rice for

top grades of sake is fairly easy to order and trace, most sake—around 65 percent of all that is made—is not premium. The rice used for that lion's share of sake on the market is cheaper than top-grade sake rice, and its cost is a driving element in the sake industry. In other words, most of the sake on the market is made of this somewhat lower-quality, significantly less-expensive rice. When the supply of that rice is threatened, the effect on the market is huge.

When brewers purchase proper sake rice for premium sake, they can order a specific variety of rice and a specific level of quality, the grade of which is assured by government inspection. But for cheap sake, there is another system in place in which brewers can request a particular variety and quality but may end up with something quite different. This is because the rice distributed under these special terms may have come from one of several sources, such as excess yields from some farmers, or rice grown under special allowances, outside of the government-imposed yearly limits.

While the cheap-sake brewer might not know exactly what he is going to get, the rice distributed to him under these terms is significantly less expensive. And at the grade of sake this rice will be used in—lower priced, less premium—the inferior quality of the rice will not make much of a difference. It will do just fine.

Rice production overall is strictly controlled by the Japanese government to avoid excess supply, which could adversely affect market stability. This control is exercised through subsidies to the farmers; in other words, the government pays them to not grow rice. These subsidies are adjusted from time to time according to policy and economic realities.

There are several governmental classifications for rice. Rice for eating, rice for sake brewing, rice for making crackers, and rice used for animal feed are all in different classifications. And the regulations for these classifications, as well as the subsidies provided for each, are subject to change. For example, farmers may be limited in how much eating rice and sake rice they can grow, but not limited in how much rice for animal feed they can grow. And they may be further motivated to grow the latter by increased subsidies for fertilizers and insecticides.

Why would the government favor something like animal-feed rice over sake rice or even rice for eating? Because limiting the need to import such rice helps offset trade imbalances, which in turn assists local agriculture. Good reasons to be sure! But the impact on sake is huge. Less availability drives up the cost of rice, which affects the brewing industry in both profitability and the price to the consumer.

More recently, the government is encouraging and subsidizing farmers to grow other crops rather than other types of rice. As policies and economics change, the farmers find more and more options, gaps, and loopholes, which can seriously affect how much rice is available to the sake-brewing industry. In truth, farmers do try to cooperate, but the government has imposed an imperfect system that calls for constant adjustments. Note that not everyone is affected. A few large and stable breweries have enough buying power to negotiate cheap-enough prices for high-enough volumes where such issues of subsidies and quotas are not a concern. They are more or less immune.

While the above discussion is related mostly to the supply of inexpensive rice for inexpensive sake, remember that this makes up most of the sake market. For high-quality sake rice for premium sake, similar problems also exist.

For example, growing rice for eating is simpler, and yields are higher than for sake rice. It can be therefore be challenging to convince farmers to grow any sake rice at all. This is why some producers have direct contracts with growers; it ensures a bit more security for both, albeit at a higher cost.

Also, remember that brewers have to buy all that rice up front. Which means every autumn, many have to strain their finances significantly just to start the season, the return on which they will not begin to see for at least a year. Securing backing and financial support in a fragile economy for a contracting industry is another big issue.

There are more vagaries that the rice-growing cartels—er, communities—employ, and often the sake brewers themselves do not fully understand them. I remember one brewer from Shiga, near Kyoto, telling me that they were finally able to grow Yamada Nishiki in Shiga.

"You mean, you could not grow it here before?" I asked inquisitively. "But I know I have had Shiga sake made with Shiga-grown Yamada Nishiki." "Well," he stammered, "you can, but you could not put it on the label—until now."

"Oh? Who controls that?" I asked. Rice growing is controlled by one industry, sake labeling by another. I sensed a disconnect. And so did he.

He thought a second, and said, "Wow. I don't know. That's just what the farmers told me. Let me check on that and get back to you!"

Yet another brewer from Yamagata told me that he had been told that one could not put the name of the rice on the label unless the seeds came from an official source (i.e., the cooperative). Huh? Says who? And enforced by whom?

"Is this the law?" I asked. "It's, uh, vague," said my Yamagata brewer friend. "And the frustrating thing is that the folks distributing the rice keep it that way. Those that know keep it vague! I could explore it further and challenge it, but I have other, higher priorities. So we just deal with it," he acquiesced.

Politics and vagueness aside, sometimes it is just a matter of pure economics. Yamaguchi Prefecture in the southwest part of Japan uses a sake rice unique to that area called Saito no Shizuku. A local *toji* explained to me how much trouble he had getting it.

"It's hard for me to develop a product using this rice because I'm not sure I will be able to get the amount I need each year, much less be able to procure an increasing amount. It is not a particularly expensive rice; in fact, it costs about the same as Gohyakumangoku," he said. "However, the per-acre yields of Gohyakumangoku are much higher, so the farmer makes more. And while the yields of my Saito no Shizuku are about the same as Yamada Nishiki, the latter garners a much higher price on the market. So I'm having trouble getting farmers to grow it for me," he lamented. Simple economics applied to sake rice. Who among us would not do the same thing?

Sake is unique in many ways. For better or worse, the extremely high cost of the raw materials is one of those unique quirks. And the byzantine distribution system—while it serves some purposes—is yet another. Suffice it to say that procuring rice for sake in Japan is significantly different from procuring grapes for wine anywhere.

Let your understanding of this add to your appreciation of all that goes into the glass of sake before you!

THE TRUTH ABOUT

Sake Outsourcing

I recall when I was visiting a very large brewery and chatting with the president, he commented how much sake they were selling back in the early 1970s, when sake production and consumption peaked. He described a scene in the main office, where the sales force all sat at desks lined up together as in a typical Japanese office. The phone would ring.

"Don't answer it," someone would say. "It's probably an order. We don't have the sake to fill it!" In other words, they could sell more than they could make back in those days, in the golden age of sake.

This was not the only company with this conundrum; back then, many of the larger brewers were in the same boat. They could sell more than they could make; they just did not have the production capacity. So they outsourced.

Outsourcing still happens today, although not to the extent it once did. A brewer would buy sake in bulk from small brewers, bringing it in tankers to their own factories (somehow the word *brewery* does not quite fit here) to bottle and sell as their own. In effect, they bought whole tanks of sake at once.

This is known as *okegai*, "tank buying," or from the opposite end of the deal, *oke-uri*, "tank selling." The well-oiled sales machines of the big companies had the resources to drum up more and more clients, but there was not enough sake to go around, at least not from their own factory. They solved the problem by approaching smaller brewers in the nearby countryside and offering to buy entire tanks of sake.

"Just brew it like this, and we will buy almost everything you make," the small brewers were told.

This symbiotic relationship worked (and still works) quite well in many senses. The large brewers got their sake, and the smaller brewers got hassle-free revenue: no bottling, marketing, or sales required. Eventually, however, things got a bit out of control, and it was estimated that at the peak of sake production and consumption, a whopping 50 to 80 percent of the sake of the large national-brand brewers was actually made by someone else. Eventually the media and consuming public caught on, and they were none too pleased.

But in a very real sense (read: economic), this system was beneficial for both sides. There was no way the little guys could sell by themselves the volume they brewed under these arrangements, and there was no way the big

Taiten Shiragiku Junmai-shu

SHIRAGIKU SHUZO KK, OKAYAMA

A mellow and rice-graced aroma that ties well into the decidedly soft and delicately rich flavor, tinged by a moderate acidity. An outstanding example of sake made with locally (Okayama) grown Omachi rice

As did many companies in Okayama Prefecture, this brewery for years was making sake for a larger brewery in neighboring Hyogo. This symbiotic relationship was a win-win situation, but as market conditions changed the brewery slowly shifted back toward its own brand and in 1997 even changed the company name to reflect its new identity. Shiragiku means "white chrysanthemum," a flower for which the town is famous.

heavies could make enough to satiate the sales force—or the management—behind them. Also, the sake sold in this way was for the most part cheap sake. Like, very cheap sake. Because character-laden premium sake cannot be easily contracted out like this if consistency and character are to remain even remotely intact, rarely if ever does this happen with premium sake. Still, then and now, it somehow smacks of something inappropriate to many people.

There is really nothing wrong with these activities, legally or ethically. It happens all the time in just about every industry. But perhaps because sake is supposed to be a connoisseur beverage brewed by master craftsmen with time-honed skills and intuitions, *okegai/oke-uri* practices can feel a bit tainted.

While outsourcing practices did (and do) take place all over Japan, they were most common in western Japan, near the yin and yang brewing behemoths of Nada (Kobe) and Fushimi (Kyoto). Countless breweries in those two prefectures—as well as the surrounding prefectures such as Nara, Shiga, Wakayama, and Okayama, which are filled with tiny neighborhood breweries—supported the industry through the sale of sake to the large brewing companies in Nada and Fushimi. In fact, many small- to medium-sized breweries with very reputable names and very fine sake did (and do) sell a bit on the side; it provides some additional revenue and helps the big brewers to boot.

When all of this naturally enough met with public disapproval, many brewers sought to distance themselves from the image of outsourced sake. A type of sake known as *ki-ippon* was born. When the word *ki-ippon* is on the bottle, it indicates that all of the sake therein was brewed at only one place. It may seem like a superfluous term to put on a label, but keep in mind the purpose was for the brewer to go out of its way to show the contents were not outsourced. These days, the term *ki-ippon* is rarely seen, and even more rarely does it retain its original meaning, having transformed itself into an indicator of overall quality.

But things are changing, mightily and fast. Breweries engaging in outsource buying and selling have dwindled in numbers, for a variety of reasons. For one, consumption of cheap sake is dropping fast. This in turn means large brewing factories can handle the demand themselves. Also, many of the smaller brewers that formerly survived on selling whole tanks of sake to large producers are now brewing their own brands and styles with a renewed sense of pride and plenty of vigor. This, in turn, gives us consumers a few more fine brands to seek out and enjoy.

In an interesting twist, in recent years the process has been reversing itself in some isolated instances. There are tiny breweries that, for example, saw their brewing staff retire before securing their successors but who still had a dedicated customer base of locals. These places would then buy sake from a large brewery that is chugging along below full capacity, slap their own labels on it, and voila! Product! While situations like this are not that common, one does hear of them from time to time.

There are many positive aspects and examples of sake outsourcing. Frequently the larger brewers foster relationships with their supplying breweries, closely supervising production to ensure the outsourced sake is brewed to exacting standards and with the requisite attention to detail. Often yeast is handed over to the outsourced brewers, which they are permitted to use in their own sake as well. This helps the smaller suppliers learn how to brew fine sake, which benefits them in the long run.

Okegai and *oke-uri* outsourcing is no longer a big or sensitive issue in the sake world. It is an important part of sake history and still takes place, although not nearly as much as it once did. And it is not likely to be practiced by anyone you know.

Sake Glassware

Surprisingly, in Japan, there is nothing remotely resembling official or proper glassware for regular sake drinking. The sake industry never got together on this one as the wine world did long ago. While a lot of good vessel options exist, there really aren't any that are officially recognized or universally accepted and recommended by the industry.

The shape and size of a vessel will drastically affect how you taste sake. The most commonly touted and most easily understood reason for this is that the human tongue senses different flavors in different regions. Sweetness, for example, is sensed on the tip of the tongue, with acidity and tartness on the sides, and bitterness in the center. Recent research has shown that, actually, we can sense all flavors all over the tongue and also that most people do indeed exhibit the above-described patterns.

So, a glass with a narrow-diameter opening will focus more of the sake onto the tip of your tongue, intensifying what sweetness there is. Similarly, a wide-mouthed glass will spread the sake out so that more of it hits the sides, potentially exaggerating its acidic qualities.

Clearly, there is more to this. Bigger glasses allow more aromatics to hover above the liquid, but more alcohol fumes as well. These have different relative weights and will settle into layers in time, so which size is best depends greatly on the character of the beverage. To me, the thickness of the rim of the glass is extremely important—I feel thinner is unequivocally better. The surface area exposed and the presence or lack of a tapering shape to the glass are all very real factors with very real effects.

Considering all this, it is just not possible to have one perfect glass for all sake. No way.

What, then, should we use when drinking sake? Well, regular wine glasses or even sherry glasses work great. They are simple, they are elegant, and they are everywhere. They hold a decent amount, and they accentuate lively, aromatic profiles wonderfully. If you have wine or sherry glasses you need not agonize about what to use for your sake. They are a great option.

However, wine glasses are not that commonly used for enjoying sake in Japan. Admittedly, long-stemmed wine glasses just don't jibe well with Japanese table settings. And Japan in any case has its own preferred vessels and glassware that have long part of its traditional sake culture. First but not foremost are

Masumi Yumedono "Mansion of Dreams" Daiginjo
MIYASAKA JOZO KK, NAGANO

Melon juicy peach aromas transition to discernible layers of textured flavor.

The company has two breweries in mountainous Nagano Prefecture that brew a fairly wide range of sake styles. This particular *daiginjo* is a brilliant example of how an aromatic and complex sake can be even more enjoyable in a wine glass than in more traditional sake glassware. The aromas are more focused and easily recognizable, and the complex flavors meld well. You may wonder why you'd ever use any other glass for sake again.

those ubiquitous little cups that are filled from narrow-topped flasks. Known as *o-choko* and *tokkuri* respectively, these are the most common implements seen for drinking cheap, hot sake. Their form follows function. A very real and pleasant custom in Japan, and one of the few "rules" surrounding sake, is that one does not pour for oneself, but rather for others, and is then poured for in return. It is a show of everything good from respect to friendship. Tiny little cups further the cause by calling for frequent refilling.

Those who love their sake also commonly use traditional Japanese pottery of a higher grade than the above-mentioned knock-offs. Japan has one of the richest ceramics cultures in the world, with styles running the gamut from rough, unglazed, and earthy to shiny, glazed, and elegant. Each piece begs a particular season, a sake style, and situation. There is no end to this world.

This pottery, however, might not focus the aromas and flavors in the same way as some other shapes, sizes, and materials. It might not be the best choice for premium sake, in particular something like a fruity *daiginjo*—at least not technically. But the tactile, visual, and cultural aspects of enjoying fine sake in fine Japanese ceramics enhance the experience immensely.

Another very common implement used to enjoy fine sake are official *kiki-choko*, or slightly smaller facsimiles of these. If well made, these round tumblers with a bold blue bull's eye pattern emblazoned on the bottom make excellent choices for tasting sake.

Kiki-choko are made of white porcelain, are fairly thin-lipped, and hold 180cc (about 6 ounces) of liquid. They are used in many if not most formal tastings and have been for about the past hundred years. The bright white porcelain allows the clear-to-amber color of the sake to be easily seen, the size allows ample room for aromatics to waft up, and the thin lip and big mouth allow sake to be well distributed about the palate, maximizing sensory input.

What of the bright-blue bull's eye pattern on the bottom? What function follows this form? While not a problem any more, long ago some sake ended up going south during storage, becoming murky to some degree in both flavor and appearance. By looking at where the blue met the white and determining how clear or diffused that border appeared, judges and assessors could tell if the sake was being stored properly.

Kiki-choko are not very commonly seen outside of the industry. You may occasionally run across them at good sake pubs, but they all look the same and smack of officialdom, and so are often eschewed for less effective but more artistic ware.

Simple tumblers are used at many a sake pub and mimic the functions of *kiki-choko*. Plain, sturdy, and straight walled, they may not amplify aromas as well as a wine glass, but they do a great job of opening up the flavors of a less ostentatious sake like a *junmai-shu*, and certainly do not dampen aromas at all. They therefore have the advantage of putting all sake on the same playing field.

Another traditional imbibing implement is a wooden box called a *masu* that holds the same amount as the official *kiki-choko* cups mentioned above, 180cc. Until half a century or so ago, these were very, very common vessels for enjoying sake. But back then, sake was brewed in wooden tanks, and until as late as the 1930s, sake was stored in wooden casks during shipment to the retailer. So serving sake like that in wood would do it no harm. But today's *ginjo* sake is best enjoyed out of other, less interfering materials. In other words, if you drink refined and aromatic *ginjo* from wooden boxes, the wood wins, the sake loses.

Interestingly, *masu* were originally a standard measure for rice and were used at every rice shop in the country as standard-sized scoops. The wood used to make *masu* is *sugi* (cryptomeria), the same wood that was formerly used in sake-brewing tanks and storage casks. As cool as they might be, your sake will likely taste better in other implements.

A wide range of cups and glasses are used for enjoying sake, and proper pottery in particular can really enhance the cultural aspects of the experience. But the last thing I want to happen is for someone interested in trying sake to forgo the chance for lack of proper glassware. It doesn't exist. Grab a wine glass, a sherry glass, or a simple tumbler and get tasting.

Milling

Earlier we learned the legal definitions of the various grades of sake. In a nutshell, *daiginjo* and *junmai daiginjo* need to be made with rice milled to 50 percent or less of its original size, *ginjo* and *junmai ginjo* to 60 percent or less, and *honjozo* to 70 percent or less. *Junmai-shu* does not have any minimum, although its *seimai-buai* must be listed on the label.

These days, as more and more information is provided to us on labels or the internet, it is not uncommon to find a sake that—based on its *seimai-buai*—could be classified as a higher grade. For example, we might see a *junmai* made with rice milled to 59 percent. This *could* be labeled a *junmai ginjo*. Or perhaps we'll find a *ginjo* made with rice milled to 48 percent. This has every legal right to be called a *daiginjo*. Why in the world would a brewer decide to not assess a sake as the highest grade for which it qualifies?

First of all, remember that the numbers representing the milling rates needed to qualify for the various grades of premium sake are minimums. While the rice only needs to be milled down to 60 percent of its original size for regular *ginjo*, it can be taken much further, and it often is. It is not at all uncommon to find top–class *daiginjo* made with a *seimai-buai* of 35 percent, meaning that 65 percent of the outside part of each grain of rice was milled away. So, milling more than the minimum requirement is something that happens often. But why would a brewer not call a sake the highest grade allowed?

The answer lies in the fact that premium sake classifications like *ginjo* and *daiginjo* are as much about a feeling as they are about rules, if not more. At least when it comes to this kind of thing, sake brewers are much more about the spirit of the law than the letter.

Rather than worrying about the number, brewers will mill the rice as far as necessary in order to reach the flavor profile they are targeting for a given product. Just how far that is will vary by producer, and by product as well. A producer might have two or more sake of any one class, each with a different *seimai-buai*. But to get the profile he is aiming for, he will mill the rice as far as is needed. If that means going into *daiginjo* territory when this is just a *ginjo*, then so be it! The number itself is secondary.

By milling down to certain level, the brewer earns the right to call it a certain grade but is not burdened with the obligation to do so. It's all a matter of image, really.

I recall visiting the *kura* brewing Rihaku in Shimane Prefecture a few years ago. The brewery had been asked by a large department-store chain to brew a *daiginjo* from rice with a 50 percent *seimai-buai*, presumably with a price point in mind—which is admittedly always an important factor. Now this fully—if barely—qualifies as a *daiginjo*. Mr. Tanaka, the owner, shook his head slowly as he gazed out the *kura* window, explaining it to me. "I did it, but I dunno, a *daiginjo* at 50 percent . . . I'm not all that comfortable with that!" To him, to have a sake be worthy of the Rihaku Daiginjo title, it had to be milled more than the bare minimum.

Not all brewers feel that way, of course. To get a *ginjo* to feel like what their *ginjo* should feel like, one brewer may only need to mill the rice to 60 percent, especially if it is a fuller sake, or (quite frankly) if their target market and price point dictate as such. Another may need to mill the rice much further, way into the legal *daiginjo* range, to feel the same level of warmth and fuzziness about their product in its target market.

This is one reason why you might sometimes see, for example, a *ginjo* that is more expensive than a *daiginjo* on the same shelf. It is possible that the rice for the *ginjo* was milled more than the rice for the *daiginjo*. The producer of the former, for a myriad of possible reasons, preferred to call his product a *ginjo*, whereas the maker of the latter was comfortable selling his as a *daiginjo*.

There are, of course, other reasons that the *ginjo* could be more expensive, including having been made with much better and more expensive rice, or with more labor-intensive processes. Perhaps it has to do with the economies of scale of the two companies involved. I think this can be confusing to some. I have on several occasions seen people shy away from a *ginjo*,

Shichihonyari Junmai Wataribune 77%

TOMITA SHUZO YG, SHIGA

A subtle, almost tickling sweetness pervades the flavor, and herbal notes complete the package, providing great overall balance.

Whereas many *daiginjo* today are made with comparatively (and competitively) higher and higher milling rates, a few—like this sake—go in the opposite direction and mill much less than the industry norms, with fascinating results. The *seimai-buai* is 77 percent, meaning only the other 23 percent was milled away. The brewery is one of the oldest in Japan and is embracing the present with passion, tradition, and bold confidence.

muttering, "If I am going to pay that much, I want a *DAIginjo*, not just a *ginjo!*"

This is perhaps not the best way to make decisions on sake, nor is basing a decision on the *seimai-buai* alone. There is far too much overlap between the grades to get overly concerned about those demarcations. In the end, sake grades are more about image and principle than bragging rights and rules.

It seems to me that far too much attention is paid to milling anyway. Sure, from a technical standpoint as well as a legal one, more milling is better; sake made with more highly milled rice is of a higher technical quality. But sometimes, "*Ginjo*, schminjo."

We should all be drinking the sake, not the label.

Pairing Sake and Food in Japan

Food pairing is such an important part of enjoying wine that many labels suggest pairings, and almost anyone handling the bottle between producer and customer will have something intelligent to say about it. That same vibe has come to be a part of sake enjoyment as well, and a very valid vibe it is.

Often I like to let the sake speak for itself, keep the food simple, and not worry about the pairing too much. This can be done with sake quite easily—it asks little of food and goes fairly well with a very wide range of choices. Sake rarely clashes with anything. Still, it holds endless promise for pairing properly and enjoyably, and it's fun to experiment with sake and cuisine from all over the world.

When sake and food comes up, people often want to know how they do it in Japan. Are there any "red with meat, white with fish" generalities used with sake? How far do they take it? How *do* they pair sake and food in Japan?

The truth is, very commonly, they don't. At least not traditionally.

I think even a hundred years ago in Paris a good restaurant would have a whole list of wines, rather than just one or two. But even today, although in recent years the situation is changing, if you go into a fine Japanese restaurant in Tokyo serving traditional food, you will find only one or two sake—one earmarked for hot, one for cold.

This is not the sake's fault! Sake certainly

has the potential for precise, well-thought-out pairings that enhance both the food and the sake. It's just that this isn't the way things were done for most of sake's history. The food—the raw materials, the preparation, and *oh*, the presentation—were the star of the show, with sake relegated to a supporting role. It needn't have been this way, but the truth is that it has been.

The thinking is, "We've got your back. Enjoy the food; we will take care of the sake for you." And it seems to have worked well enough. I recall once going into a sushi shop in Tokyo at which I was a regular, or at least enough of one to tease the guy behind the counter. I inquired as to why he only had one sake on hand.

"Listen, smart-ass," he said in not quite those words, "I was up at four in the morning today to go to Tsukiji to buy twenty-six different kinds of fish. For you. Do you think I want you paying attention to the sake? Pay attention to the fish; I will handle the sake for you!" When put that way, it does sort of make sense!

So, pairing sake and food has not been nearly as active a sport in Japan as pairing wine and food has been in the Western world. Moreover, while it is more and more common to create wonderful food and sake pairings, there is no proper or authentic way of doing it. Nor is there any consensus throughout the industry on how it should be done.

There are, of course, various philosophies and systems that have been developed; many are solid and practical. They can be quite helpful, but as good as they might be, none has been around for very long, and none has been universally agreed upon or adopted by the industry as a whole. It's kind of hard to call something just invented last year a "traditional" approach. In that sense, there really is no authentic or traditional approach to pairing sake and food in Japan.

What is good about this is that there are

no rules to break, no traditions to violate, no generalizations to which we must adhere.

It's not as if everyone was lazy all these centuries, never bothering to develop practices and approaches to pairing sake and food. If we look at how most sake was enjoyed in Japan for so long, we can see that sake was serving its purpose just fine. People (in particular, men, who drank the biggest share of sake) enjoyed sake with small nibbles, most commonly salty and packed with umami. These varied from region to region, and the sake was more or less made to accompany them. So, small, salty dishes with local brew went quite well.

After the sake part of the evening, the men would move on to finishing up with rice, miso soup, and pickles, at which point the sake was commonly cleared from the table. The entire Japanese way of enjoying sake and food was a bit different from the West's, and thus, pairing

Mizbasho "Early Bloom" Ginjo
NAGAI SHUZO KK, GUNMA

Peach, apple, and banana in the alluring aromas and flavors, with a soft overall profile that leans slightly on the sweet side but with lots and lots of depth.

Mizbasho (aka Mizubasho) is incredibly versatile with a wide range of both Western and Japanese food. Grilled white fish or scallops bring out umami in the sake, slightly sweet sauces encourage a similar sweetness to develop, and the light softness helps it pair with a melon-like dessert or amuse-bouche. Carpaccio to yakitori, lemon-drizzled grilled pork to baked salmon, and even lime sherbet all invite this *ginjo* to companionship.

developed differently. There are many other reasons, but this is an important one.

Things in Japan are changing for the better, and quickly. More and more modern Japanese restaurants offer a sizable list of sake with their food and are developing some conventions of active pairing and recommendations. While there is still some catching up to do, matching sake with food can be enjoyable and interesting, done with precision and with great success.

So, how does one go about it? What are at least some rules or principles? What are the goals? It's not rocket science. You look for flavors, aromas, and other aspects of the sake and the food that are a little bit similar so they dovetail nicely, or that contrast well so as to bring out particular aspects. The goal is simple: make the sake and the food taste better together through similarities or contrasts in flavor, and elevate the overall experience of enjoying them together. That's it.

One thing that holds people back is the idea that sake needs to be paired with Japanese food. "Well, we're not having sushi tonight, so why would we have sake?" Even if they do pair sake with something other than sushi, if they go so far as to leave the realm of Japanese food and foray into pairing sake with Western cuisine, people are often overly concerned about doing it right. Folks want to know "how they do it in Japan." But there is no one right way, so there are no traditions to violate. It's liberating, really.

On a more practical level, sake truly does go well with a wide range of food. It may be the most versatile beverage on the planet in that regard. Sake has comparatively low acidity and zero tannins, making clashes very avertable. Obviously there will be some things that will not work, some foods that will clash with sake or simply drown it out with overwhelming flavors. Heavy, rich sauces or seasonings are tough

Pairing Sake and Food in Japan

139

with sake, as is really spicy food (although you should try *nigori* sake with Thai food!). But depending on how it is prepared, sake shows potential affinity with everything from vegetables and fish to chicken and pork, and even beef can work well if done right. It really is hard to have a total mismatch.

A handful of ideas off the cuff include *namazake* with raw vegetables with a bit of bitterness to them; a rich, dry *junmai* with bolstering, fat-cutting acidity paired with a cream-based sauce sprinkled with bacon over pasta; and a sweeter sake with salty, grilled salmon. Grilled lamb and *yamahai* is a match made in heaven, thanks to the slight gaminess they share. Simple, clean, slightly aromatic *ginjo* with white-flesh sashimi would qualify as a last meal on this planet for me.

Dessert sake are harder to come by, partly because most traditional Japanese desserts are not nearly as intense in their sweetness as their Western counterparts, and they were often created with green tea in mind. It is said in Japan that those who like sake do not generally like sweet things; perhaps this thinking is part of it. But *kijoshu* (sake made using already completed sake in place of some water) is a style that has the sweetness for that task.

Cheese can be quite fun to experiment with, and often aged sake offers great potential, as does earthy sake or sake with prominent acidity. Although not very common, sake made with white or black strains of *koji* (rather than the usual yellow *koji*) present types of acid that are more dark and intense, and these often go well with aged cheese.

The possibilities are truly endless. It is just a matter of experimentation.

There are, however, some noticeable differences in how you might select a sake for pairing from how you might select a wine—some methods that might work occasionally with wine are best avoided when choosing sake. It is hard to pair a sake just from the information on the label.

Let's look at region, for example. While sake does have some regionality, it is not nearly as clearly delineated as it is in the wine world. Choosing sake by region leaves too much potential error for comfort. The same is true when selecting a sake by the rice variety. While different rice types do have particular characteristics that can be associated with them, two *toji* can take the same rice milled down to the same degree and make two totally different sake. Rice variety alone is not enough information to safely make a pairing.

Nor is grade. While pairing by grade is probably the safest of these three, there is so much overlap between the various grades of sake in terms of style and typical aromas and flavors that this system has its major shortcomings too.

In the end, the most reliable way to know how to pair a sake is to taste it. Forget the label; smell it and taste it, look at aromas, flavors, acidity, intensity, texture, breadth, weight, and more. Then consider which aspects will dovetail or contrast in mutually complementary ways with your food.

Most important, do not be afraid to violate perceived authenticity. Do not limit yourself by saying, "I want to do it the way they do it in Japan." Violate away! And enjoy sake's incredible pairing potential with food.

Women in *Kura*

Whenever we hear about a *toji*, or master brewer, almost exclusively the word "he" is used. That's because almost all the *toji* in the sake world are men. And not just the *toji*. Almost all the *kura-bito* (brewing staff working under a *toji*) are men as well.

Things are surely changing; today it is rare to find a brewery that does not have women involved in brewing to some degree, and there are even a handful of women *toji* out there as well. But twenty to thirty years ago, this would not have been the case at all.

How did this state of affairs come about? It's just the way Japan has always been, and not just the sake world. Have you ever seen a female sushi chef? Most likely not, but why? Rumor has it that women's hands are warmer than men's—too warm to handle the fish. But in reality, it just isn't done, and there are no good reasons.

Sumo is also closed to women; women cannot even set foot on the clay ring in which the wrestlers compete, or it must be destroyed and rebuilt.

There are many other examples, and most are as groundless in their reasoning as the explanations surrounding the historical and traditional absence of women in *sakagura*. For example, some suggest that women's perfume and cosmetics would get into the *koji* or the yeast and affect the final sake. Or, some simply say that a woman's presence would contaminate the sake—scientific grounds be damned.

However, there are a couple of reasons that

do hold some remote semblance of sound logic, "remote" being the key word here.

Long ago, all *kurabito* were farmers or fishermen that came to the *kura* to live for anywhere from three to six months. They would leave their wives and families at home, and there would be twenty to thirty men living, working, and sleeping shoulder to shoulder in the *kura* for the duration of the brewing season. Teamwork was essential to their success. Personal differences had to be mutually respected. Distractions had to be minimized.

Many believe that the mood within the brewery will dictate how the sake ends up, and that the personality of the brewer, *toji*, and *kurabito* has a tangible effect on the flavors, aromas, and nature of the sake. There is an expression, *wajo-ryoshu*, the four characters of which mean "harmony, brew, good, sake." And so harmony among the brewing staff is key.

Consider a situation in which there are a bunch of young men working for three to six months in the brewery. If a young woman wanders in, this could get the men thinking. They may miss their wife and family and become distracted from the task at hand. Or perhaps petty jealousies arise. Expect the quality of the sake to take a big hit from lack of harmony from that point on, since the micro-organisms will sense the competitive stress and be affected. Or so goes the thinking of the ancients.

Of course, concessions were made in response to necessity. During World War II, when there were almost no young men left to do what little brewing was taking place at the time, women sometimes stepped into the *kura* to keep the family business going until the men came home. Then, as societal changes led to fewer young people willing to live half the year away from their families, further shrinking the pool of potential *kurabito*, women in *kura* became more commonplace.

Some *kura* maintained the ban on women,

or vestigial remnants of it, for years. I recall visiting a brewery with my wife in the late '90s. As one of the underlings set out to take us around, we were warned by the president, "Try to avoid the *toji*; he doesn't like women in the brewery."

But this situation has almost completely changed. While I would not say women in sake breweries are now common, I would say their presence is no big deal. There are perhaps thirty women *toji*, and rare is the brewery that does not have women involved in some part of the production process. There are even a couple staffed by more women than men.

So while the use of the masculine pronoun may end up being factually correct most of the time, women *toji* are not the unthinkable chimeras they once were. If anything, they are more like celebrities these days, which is closer to how things should be.

SAKE SELECTION

Moon on the water
Fukucho Junmai ginjo

Fukucho "Moon on the Water" Junmai Ginjo

IMADA SHUZO KK, HIROSHIMA

Unique licorice-tinged aromas, full then astringently tapering flavor.

Miho Imada did not originally intend to become one of only a handful of female *toji*. But circumstances led to her heading home to Hiroshima from Tokyo to help out and eventually take over the family sake-brewing business. First things first: the master brewer needed a successor. So she worked under him long enough to be able to take over on her own, and has indeed made her mark with creativity and a unique style.

THE
BREWER'S
ART
REVEALED

Koji Making

Koji making is the heart of the sake-brewing process. Nothing holds as much sway over the nature of the final sake—in both positive attributes and potential negative ones—as how the *koji* was made or, in other words, how the mold *Aspergillus oryzae* was coaxed to grow onto and into the steamed rice.

In explanations of how sake is made, we often hear, "And then this mold is grown on about 20 to 25 percent of the rice, and that provides enzymes for starch-to-sugar conversion," as if it were a straightforward step or process. Perish the thought!

To review, brewing a tank of sake starts with a yeast starter (the *moto*): a small tank in which *koji*, steamed rice, and water are mixed and then dosed with yeast. After this chugs along for two weeks, more *koji*, steamed rice, and water are added three times over four days. It is done this way, rather than all at once, to maintain the correct balance of sugar content and yeast needed to encourage long-term, healthy fermentation.

So, *koji* is used four times across the twenty- to forty-day brewing process, and every single time the *koji* making takes place, it happens differently. It is bewilderingly complicated and very much an art as well as a skill.

For example, consider the strength of the enzymes, determined by—among other things—the amount of mold applied to the rice. This might be 30 grams per every 100 kilograms of steamed rice (more or less, depending on various factors). However, for each of the three successive additions, less and less mold is used as fewer enzymes are needed. So for every one batch of sake, the *koji* can be made up to four different ways.

Then there is the grade of sake. *Koji* for the rough, twenty-day fermentation used for cheap *futsu-shu* is made completely differently from *koji* made for *ginjo* or *daiginjo*. The main difference is TLC—attention to the details. But if a brewer makes ten different products, which is very common, then that would be ten different ways of making *koji*, times four of course.

Beyond this, how *koji* is made will vary from rice to rice since different varieties behave differently in terms of how hard or soft they are, and how they dissolve. This also changes each year based on things like the weather and the whims of the sake-brewing gods. And of course, *koji* must be handled in an appropriate way for each different milling rate as well.

Not to be forgotten is the general style of

Kikuyoi Ginjo

AOSHIMA SHUZO KK,
SHIZUOKA

Deliberately subdued aromas of apple, melon and banana intertwined into a pleasant package, and a full, clean flavor profile, low in acidity and decidedly not ostentatious. Drinking it is like hanging out with an old friend.

The *toji* here is the son of the current president, and his passion and attention to detail in brewing are unsurpassed. Whereas most *koji* takes about 48 hours to make, here it takes 70 hours. And the *toji* checks on the temperature and moisture every 90 minutes, night and day. What this means is that he does not sleep longer than 90 minutes at a stretch between October and April. Ever.

the sake being made. Sake with heavier, sweeter, or richer flavor profiles inherit those qualities from the *koji*, as does sake with lighter more delicate styles. It is all in how the mold is grown.

Considering the factors of rice, milling rate, year, grade, flavor profile, and stage of the process, we see the permutations are endless, which is why it is not an exaggeration to say that the *koji* is made differently *every single time*.

Other differences beyond the strength of the starch-to-sugar converting enzymes might be the moisture of the completed *koji*. Some steps and some sake call for heavy, moist *koji* whereas others use *koji* that is hard and quite dry. This affects how fast the *koji* will dissolve in the fermenting mash, and therefore how sugar will be injected, and how much.

The craftsman can also control just where on the rice the mold grows. Some sake will call for letting the mold grow richly and opulently around the outside of the grain, but others need to have the mold grow less on the surface and more toward the center of the grain. Oversimplifying, the former method is more commonly used for heavier sake, the latter for lighter sake and *ginjo* sake.

How does one orchestrate the growth of mold on several million grains of rice under his or her tutelage at one given time to be on the outside or the inside of the rice grains? By using moisture and humidity.

Mold likes moisture. If the humidity in the special, wooden-walled *koji*-making room is high, the outside of the rice grains remains moist. The mold feels no need to go anywhere and just grows around the surface. But if the room is dried out and the humidity drops significantly, provided the rice is regularly mixed well enough, then the outside surface will dry out too. This sends the mold into a tizzy, and it starts to grow in toward the center of the grains, where it senses more moisture.

The *koji*-making rooms have elaborate

ventilation systems that allow the workers to minutely mix the air inside the room with that from the outside, thus adjusting and controlling humidity. I have seen brewers make an incredibly small, several-centimeter adjustment in the size of the ventilation aperture, barely noticeable to most. Their years of experience and refined senses have taught them that tweaks like that will make the final sake taste better.

As used, the word *koji* refers to rice with mold already carefully propagated upon it, while the mold itself is called *koji-kin* (*koji* mold). Although *koji-kin* occurs naturally in the air, brewers in Japan buy it from one of about five specialty mold producers in Japan. It can be propagated again and again like sourdough, but instead brewers use a fresh dose of mold spores each and every time. There are perhaps a dozen strains of *koji* mold available to brewers from each of the companies that supply the industry. Of course, the strain of mold is important, but the real secret—the real important difference— is in how the mold itself is propagated onto and into the rice. The methods and skills are more important than the strain of mold itself.

Koji is used for many other things outside of sake in traditional Japanese cuisine, most notably miso and *shoyu* (soy sauce). Long ago there were businesses that did nothing but make and sell *koji* to townsfolk who made their own miso at home.

An expression in the sake-brewing world goes, *Ichi—koji, ni—moto, san—tsukuri*. First in importance is making good *koji*, next comes making the yeast starter, and third comes the fermentation. That's how important *koji* making is.

Koji: it is *not* just moldy rice.

THE TRUTH ABOUT

Toji

Over the centuries, and across the many stages of sake's development, the people who brewed sake have changed. As economic and social factors in Japan congealed into the stable feudal system that lasted a millennium or so, *sakagura* (sake breweries) commonly came to be owned by wealthy or aristocratic landowner families. These families often conducted commerce in several arenas, one of which might be making sake.

But the owning family, the *kuramoto*, did not brew the sake themselves. Not for them the dirtying of hands or toiling the long hours! The actual brewing was done by craftsmen, mostly farmers from predominantly snowy regions who worked their land all spring, summer, and fall but were more or less snowbound and idle during the winter months. A wonderfully symbiotic (for that era) relationship developed in which these folks would travel some distance from their homes and work in a sake brewery for as much as six months during the cold seasons and trek back home in the spring. The same group would return to the same *kura* the next fall, and the cycle would continue the same way each year. This provided them with much-needed income when they were without work and gave the *kura* owners the work force they needed, and only during the time they needed it.

Within the group of workers that came to a brewery each year, there was of course one guy in charge, and he was the *toji*.

Just what is a *toji*? In short, a master brewer.

There might be anywhere from four to forty people brewing sake at a given *kura*, but there is only one *toji*, with all the workers under him known as *kurabito*, or "people of the *kura*." Traditionally, the *toji* was the decision maker. He called the shots, and the quality of the sake depended heavily on his skill, decisiveness, and innovations. It was his expertise, experience, and intuition that would make or break a sake and the reputation of the *kura* that produced it. As such, *toji* have long been respected or even revered, laden with massive responsibility, and storied in folklore and tradition.

Until a couple of decades ago, the *toji* was always a man, but these days there are a good number of women *toji* as well.

The term *toji* is just a title. If you are the guy in charge at a given brewery, you are the *toji*. That's it. No official certification is necessary, although some programs do exist. However, a

Yuho "Yama-oroshi" Junmai Kimoto
MIOYA SHUZO KK, ISHIKAWA

Rich honey-lemon nose. Dry and umami-filled flavor, smooth and fine grained, less acidity than one would expect from the aromas.

Most *toji* are career brewers and traditionally had to toil for many years under another *toji*, slowly stealing enough secrets to master the necessary skills. Not this guy. Toshiaki Yokomichi used to be a sake-loving employee of the Osaka school system. In the early 90s, at age 31, he joined a sake brewery and very quickly, after working for just a few years, became one of the most skilled *toji* of his guild, the Noto guild.

person does not normally come upon that title or position until he or she has accrued years and years of experience and demonstrated the requisite ability to manage the job.

A good *toji* possesses an amazingly well-honed set of skills. Making sake, and especially making great sake, cannot be done by the book. The stuff has a life of its own, quite literally. How it develops is a function of countless factors, like this year's rice crop, weather, the harmony (or lack thereof) between brewing personnel, and more. Factoring all these in, and then knowing when to lower the temperature or raise it, how to minutely adjust this or that, and what precise moment to press away the ambrosia from the fermenting mash, all calls for a focus combined with a sixth sense that is not found in the average individual.

The craftsmen on this level have very highly refined senses, and the sight, taste, and smell of a fermenting mash will tell them more than a thermometer, hydrometer, or any other instrument. A finger dipped in a tank is more reliable than a computer-controlled temperature gauge. The sound of a bubbling, fermenting mash is more revealing than that day's chemical measurement of alcohol or specific gravity.

Is every *toji* like this? Heavens no, of course not. Many just get by, as does the sake they brew. But behind every great sake is, rest assured, a great *toji*.

Historically *toji* were seasonal employees with a recurring six-month contract, but even so there has always been great loyalty between *toji* and *kuramoto*. Sure, there are politics and friction from time to time. Even *toji* are human, after all. But more often than not a *toji* will spend most if not all of his career at one brewery. He becomes part of the family and is called *oyaji* (uncle) by the children. Are there exceptions? Yes. Famous ones. But they are the exceptions, not the rule.

Beyond the brewing responsibilities, *toji* are in charge of lots and lots of paperwork, such as filing tax reports (sake is all about taxes, mind you!), accounting for every grain of rice, and sending brewing plans that show how each grain will be used before the brewing season even begins. In fact, long ago, the *kuramoto* (brewery owner) would contract with the *toji* only. The *toji* would then choose whom to hire and fire, pay the *kurabito* (the brewery workers under his management), make all the decisions of what to brew, and often procure the rice as well. These days, the *toji* might also do sales work in the off-season. It is a job that calls for many hats.

While making tasty sake is the *toji*'s job, there are those who say that what makes a great *toji* is the ability to maintain consistency from year to year. No matter what the weather or how good or bad the rice crop, regardless of which piece of equipment breaks down at crucial junctures or what personnel problems arise, a great *toji* will navigate it all and brew sake that tastes and smells more or less the way it does each year. Consistency is important.

Sake brewing, while laborious and strenuous, is not grunt work, but rather a learned skill and craft. Not just any schmuck can do it. *Toji* have always been highly respected even back in their own towns and farming villages. Since they hailed from relatively concentrated regions around Japan, they would to some degree exchange notes and teach each other when they returned home. Over time, these *toji* formed guilds that developed reputations and influenced regional styles.

These guilds took on names that are thankfully much more interesting than "Toji Local 210" and refer to the regions from which they hail. As almost all *toji* guilds have been around for hundreds of years, the guild names are regional names that were in use before the Meiji Restoration in the late 19th century. For example, the large and well-organized Nanbu Toji guild is from Iwate Prefecture up north, which was once called the land of Nanbu. The highly respected Echigo Toji guild is centered in what used to be called the land of Echigo, but is currently Niigata Prefecture. And the Izumo Toji guild is from the ancient land of Izumo in modern-day Shimane Prefecture.

The guilds had varying degrees of organization. Some were loose groups of a few guys, while others have always been well-oiled institutions. The head of one guild told me, "Every Saturday about ten of us young brewers aiming to become *toji* would gather at my house and my dad would teach us for a couple of hours. That was the extent of it." Contrast that with the Nanbu Toji guild, that bastion of higher sake-brewing education, which has a regular, thorough, and comprehensive *toji*-training program for its active members.

This has helped the Nanbu Toji guild become the pre-eminent guild it is today. It is the only one whose number of members has not dropped over the years but has remained steady at over 370 members who are currently employed as *toji*, and about 1,400 guild members overall. It is one of only a couple of guilds that provides an official *toji* licensing program, so that some members are licensed to be *toji* even if they are not actually serving as the *toji* at their *kura* of employment.

The main three guilds in numbers and reputation are the aforementioned Nanbu and Echigo guilds, followed by the Tanba Toji guild from the Tanba region of Hyogo Prefecture. They are collectively referred to as the "Sandai" Toji (The Big Three). Other important guilds today are the Izumo Toji from Shimane, the Noto Toji from Ishikawa, the Tajima Toji also from Hyogo, and the Hiroshima Toji from Hiroshima.

Currently there are about twenty-five guilds left, but the number continues to fall.

Many are gone forever, as their membership dwindled to zero. About a century ago there were as many as ten thousand companies brewing sake in Japan; now that number has dropped to a mere 1,200 or so. Accordingly, the number of *toji* has also declined. Some guilds have just a couple members remaining. Sometimes these "associate members" are not even originally from or living in those regions, but rather belong because they worked under a *toji* from that guild.

Why is this? In short, change. These changes include changes in society, culture, and economy.

Sake brewing did not start out with the current *toji* system in place. As sake became a commercially viable product a millennium or so ago, brewers started to brew only in the cold season when the bacteria could be reined in, which led to better sake. This meant they had to brew at least twice as much to maintain the same level of production. Accordingly, their seasonal labor needs surged. They moved away from local year-round hires and toward workers who thrived on a system of a few months of live-in work with very long hours. This system worked well for centuries.

However, the system has several drawbacks. For one, brewing is quite simply hard work. Long ago, it might have been a great option for a young man, but today, there are so many other choices. One can join a sake brewery and live there six months a year, working shoulder to shoulder with the same skeleton crew every day. Or one can move to the city, live in one's own place, get a year-round job at a company, and party in Tokyo on Friday and Saturday nights. As more young folks have opted for the latter, the average age of *toji* from the guilds has steadily risen to be well into the upper sixties.

Also, historically the *toji* wielded significant power in the company. The *toji* might have commanded a salary far too high for today's mostly small business operations. The hierarchy within the confines of the *kura* could be intense too, as often the *toji* was "like a god." I recall one brewing friend of mine who had the dubious distinction of working under one of the most famous *toji* in the industry.

"I could not even speak to him directly," he lamented. "It was not until about five years after he retired that I could at last look him in the eye and talk to him."

Something interesting to note: almost never is the *toji* job handed from father to son. When a *toji* retires, commonly his number-two man will take over, or the *kuramoto* will contact the guild for a replacement. Sometimes a *toji* will properly teach his underlings so that they can continue to maintain the *kura* style after his departure, but others unfortunately take their secrets to the grave with them. Long ago, sake making was all quite secretive, and *toji* zealously guarded their brewing secrets. Today, however, this is not the case, and in the unified struggle of sake against all other alcoholic beverages, there is much more of a spirit of cooperation.

Another agent of change from the traditional system is that, often, the owner of a medium-sized family business (which is what most sake breweries are) cannot afford to put the future and livelihood of the company in the hands of just one person. "If the *toji* moves on or falls ill, we are doomed!" This is clearly not a sustainable situation for most modern companies, so things have entered a phase of accelerated change.

There is a growing trend of "owner *toji*," brewery owners that take the brewing responsibilities into their own hands. It might be the president himself, or his son or daughter, or even a local hire that spent time under the tutelage of the former *toji*, but many *kura* no longer depend on *toji* from the traditional guilds. Fortunately, many young brewers seem to be embracing this path with passionately open arms, wanting to get in there and get their hands wet and rice covered.

Locally hired *toji* may be associated with a traditional guild, but more and more *toji* are year-round (rather than seasonal) locally hired employees. While this may signify the beginning of the end for a certain traditional aspect of the sake-brewing world, it is surely the best chance of survival when all things are considered.

Hiring local people as the *kurabito* to work under the *toji* is another trend. This lets them go home most nights rather than live away from their families, making the job far more appealing to the youth of modern society. In fact, the industry has changed so much and so fast that by some estimates, today a full one-third of all sake breweries employ family members or local hires as *toji*. Since another one-third are *toji* from the Nanbu guild, the other four hundred or so are split among the remaining guilds.

Does it really matter from which guild a *toji* hails? Certainly, the guilds have their styles. But in truth these differences are subtle, and to us mortals, nah, it does not really matter. Also, a good *toji* from any guild can brew any style he or she chooses, often at the behest of the *kuramoto*. As such, the distinctions between the guilds and styles are becoming blurred, diminishing the reliance on the guilds of old.

I recall once drinking sake with two sake illuminati, one a *toji* himself, and the other a tasting genius. They were discussing a couple of *toji* from the Tanba guild, and the *toji* with whom I drank commented how the first guy did not really uphold a true Tanba style, while the other gent was indeed a quintessential representative of that guild's brewing culture.

The fine distinctions were lost on me, but at least I could understand and respect the tradition of craftsmanship behind his observation.

* * *

Confusing though they might be, here are three terms worth remembering: *kuramoto* (the brewery owner, or the owning family in general), *kurabito* (brewery workers), and *toji* (master brewer). These words are bound to come in handy the next time you visit a *sakagura*.

Why All Brewers Make All Grades

The sake industry is an equal-opportunity industry, at least in terms of product. Every producer is free to make any kind of product it likes and is not limited or relegated by region, law, or anything else. The grades are determined by how the raw materials are processed, and provided a *kura* has the money and willingness, it can make any grade it chooses. This, along with the way the industry matured throughout history, is why all brewers make all grades.

Basically, every brewer will make a *daiginjo*, a *junmai daiginjo*, and everything down to a lowly bottom-shelf *futsu-shu*. There are exceptions, of course, like *everything* in the sake world! But for the most part all brewers make most, if not all, grades of sake.

The ratios do differ from place to place. For example, a very large brewer may make 99 percent *futsu-shu*, and less than 1 percent *daiginjo*, as well as a handful of products in between. Their premium sake will be very good, as they have the wherewithal to make whatever they want to make, and their price performance will be outstanding. But the major part of their revenue will come from *futsu-shu*. Which is fine!

A very small brewer, on the other hand, might make almost all premium sake from *junmai-shu* on up, but will very commonly make a bit of *futsu-shu* to be able to put their name on a local product that has been in the 'hood forever. While they might not sell much of it, it is worth it for them to continue. Their distribution might be the opposite of a larger brewer, but they still make a little bit of everything.

Like everything in the sake world, there are a few exceptions. There are perhaps thirty places that make only *junmai-shu*, *junmai ginjo*, and *junmai daiginjo*. A few make only premium sake—no *futsu-shu*, but everything above. One or two make only *ginjo*. There are even a couple that make no *ginjo*, but only grades lower than that. This may be because the *toji* has never made anything but *futsu-shu*, perhaps to be sold off to a larger brewer, and does not have the willingness or confidence to undertake something else. If the local market for *futsu-shu* is strong (a very rare situation these days) that might suit the company fine. But a brewer with no *ginjo* might be that way because the owner is "old school" and doesn't like that modern, fruity *ginjo* stuff. All have their niche, and as long as they continue to thrive, that niche is where they will stay. That's fine too.

These examples notwithstanding, there is no such thing as a region or class of brewers that makes *ginjo*, while another stratum makes the lower grades. Everybody has their hands in everything, or at least, they can if they so choose.

The timing and flow of what is made when is interesting too. When a *toji* and the brewers enter the *kura* in October or so, they first scrub the place down and take care of other preparations. Then the first few batches they make will be *futsu-shu*, or at least the lower grades. They do this for a number of reasons. First, it is still comparatively warm out. The colder it is, the easier it is to control fermentation, so the best stuff is made in the colder months, usually around January. Also, the best sake rice is harvested later than cheaper, regular rice, so what they have to work with is not yet the best rice.

Most importantly, every year is different in terms of how the rice behaves, what the temperature is like, and other idiosyncrasies around the *kura*. No two years are the same, and by starting with the cheaper sake, a brewer can feel things out before it really matters.

How will the rice fare during milling? Will it crack and break a lot, or be sturdy and true? How well will it absorb water? Quickly or grudgingly? Sure, the weather should tell them that, but one never knows until one tries. How readily will it dissolve in the ferment-ing mash? Too slowly and the final flavors are tight and conservative, too quickly and the sake tastes rough and sloppy.

By designating the first few batches as cheaper sake, *toji* can make guesstimates and adjustments. Through trial and error, by the time the coldest part of the season rolls around the *kura* is ready for the best rice for their top grades of sake.

After that, as the weather warms up again, they often return to a last few batches of lesser

sake to wrap up the long brewing season. Just how many tanks of top-grade stuff and how many of lesser and much-lesser stuff is made will vary from *kura* to *kura*, so the timing of when things change is different at each place as well.

In practice, there are so many products that a *kura* can make. Not only can it make sake at each grade, but also at different *seimai-buai* at the same grade, with different rice types or yeasts, either pasteurized or *nama*, *genshu* (undiluted) or regular, very young, standard maturity, or aged longer than usual—the permutations are endless. While some places with the requisite energy undertake all of these, most brewers do not. Still, most have at least a horse in the race at each of the main representative grades.

DEVELOPING YOUR
SAKE-TASTING ABILITY

One of the best ways to learn, understand, and appreciate more about sake—not to mention to fuel your interest in it—is to improve and hone your sake-tasting ability, known as *kikizake-noryoku* in Japanese. Getting to the point where you can identify certain things about a sake can significantly enhance the sake experience.

Certainly, though, this is not a prerequisite to enjoying sake. In the end, it's all about personal preference. If you like it, you're done. Like they used to say in Rome back in the day, "De gustibus non est disputandum." Or, "Drink whatever you like." (Actually, it means, "In matters of taste there can be no disputes," but you get the idea.) It is enough to know what you like and to stick with it—no further intellectual efforts are needed.

But being able to pick out things like maturity, nuances related to pasteurization, textures, weights, aromas, and concrete flavors often makes it more fun and allows you to help promote sake to those you run with.

For example, knowing if a sake is too old—or on the contrary still eminently enjoyable despite an old-ish date on the bottle—and just sensing maturity as a quality or point of preference are skills well worth developing.

How can we go about doing that?

While some people are more naturally talented in areas like this, we can all learn to identify sake well, or, at the very least, improve our abilities. If we try, we can all get better.

Honing Expression and Memory

There are two things involved in learning to taste sake like a pro. One is your ability to clearly express the aromas, flavors, acidity, textures, weights, and nuances you sense. The second is your ability to remember these from moment to moment, and from sake to sake.

How do we improve those two things? The simplest if not most indispensable way is to train yourself to take tasting notes. Constantly. Every time. It will indeed call for discipline; after all, in the middle of a fun evening who wants to bother to take a note on a sake you have had many times? And if it stops being fun we defeat the purpose. But as much as possible, and especially when tasting professionally, take a note or two on each sake that you taste.

It need not be long, or complex. Start with simple descriptions: apple, acidic, thin, clean, light, textured, rich, cloying . . . all words that arise are fair game. If at first you do not have the vocabulary, or feel your current vocabulary is inadequate, or simply nothing pops into your mind, stick with it. The words will eventually come. And the physical act of jotting down your impressions will crystalize your expression about that sake.

Not just expressing observations but also writing them down will help you to remember them, which is the second skill to develop. As you stick with it, in time you will develop a general feel for particular sake brands, sake styles, and sake regions. It is a matter of memory and expression: first expressing your impressions concretely, and then remembering them.

Next, work toward associating those remembered, concrete expressions with something related to the sake. That "something" can be region, rice, maturity, yeast, grade, or individual brewers. If a sake has a particular "lightness of being" in your own words and feelings, note if it can be associated with a brewer, rice, or grade. The next time you notice that quality, if it is again from the same brewer or made with the same rice as the first one, well, then you are on to something.

Some examples might be acidity levels in *yamahai*, apple and melon in *ginjo*, earthiness in more mature sake, or herbal tones with rice types like Omachi or Hattan. The more you mess with this stuff, the more fun it gets, and the more you broaden your sake horizons.

Cultivating Consistency

Here is an important point: the goal should be reproducibility. This is what really matters. Can you sense the same thing about the same sake, or about sake that share certain qualities? If you smell peach and others smell apple, that is fine as long as each time you encounter that sake—or one of similar characteristics—you again smell peach. If you smell peach one time and licorice the next, you'll be hard-pressed to reliably assess even your own preferences.

Fortunately, there are ways of improving these abilities. One concrete method has worked very well for me. It's not exactly rocket science, but it's a good and measurable way to improve your sake-tasting skills.

Start with five identical glasses. White wine glasses are a good choice, as are wide-mouthed, simple tumblers (which would be more commonly used by pros in Japan). Find a way to unobtrusively label each one with a number from one to five. A small sticker on the bottom of the glass works well for this.

Get five different sake and place identical amounts of each into the five glasses. Place the glasses lined up in order. However you choose to align them is fine, but make it a habit from which you do not deviate and line them up the same way each time. It will make things much easier in the long run.

Now taste them, and take notes. Look at aromas, flavors, acidity, textures, and any other qualities and idiosyncrasies you can perceive.

Use water to cleanse your palate as needed. Using a spittoon is wise.

Next, mix 'em up. Just shuffle the glasses around into a different order. Play the shell game with the five glasses long enough for you to be truly confused about which sake is now in what position. Take a long, careful look at your notes from the first round, and taste them all again with those notes in mind. You know what you are looking for. Each sake you taste should smell and taste like one of the five you had in the first round. Check them off as you go.

Be sure to use the process of elimination. Certainly this is a bit of a crutch, but it helps focus your attention on what you *actually* tasted and smelled. For example, if one of the five is particularly mature or fruity and stands out, find that one first. Eliminate that as having been matched, and now you need to match but four, and you can focus your senses on what your notes say should be present in the remaining sake. For this reason, I recommend performing a quick, perfunctory sniff and a taste run-through at the start of the second round, to see what stands out.

When you are finished, check your results. How did you do? Five out of five? Zero? Three, perhaps? Regardless, stick with it. Your senses will become more refined, and you will definitely learn to taste sake better. Focus first on matching, on reproducibility. That may take time; it may not. Certainly some people will have more innate ability than others. However, everyone can improve his or her senses and abilities to taste and know sake; about this I am sure.

Tips and Tricks to Practice Tasting

We all have good tasting days and bad tasting days. Colds, allergies, fatigue, and stress will all affect our body condition, determining how well we can taste on a given day. Stick with your program, and try to practice several times a week at the minimum.

Make it as easy as you need to at first, and increase the level of difficulty with time. If five sake in your tasting is too many and makes you feel clueless, start with three instead. Work to four in time and go to five from there. When just starting out, select five sake that are vastly different in style to make distinctions easier to grasp. You can eventually work toward more similar sake to hone your abilities further. As the goal is to be able to pick out idiosyncrasies, be sure to include sake with some quirks. Get an over-the-hill sake, a *yamahai*, a fruity *daiginjo*, or a *namazake*. Vastly different flavor profiles will help you to discern those idiosyncrasies at first and then to notice them in the field or real world later.

In fact, I regularly torture sake—I leave it to oxidize or get old, or I let *nama* go a bit south of the border—to help my educational efforts. Sake that are over the hill are readily available and well worth the investment in your education.

Next, I recommend doing all you can to not allow your logical mind to grab a foothold in your tasting. Do your best to remain as clueless as possible and instead leave everything to your palate. Your logical mind will (mine does, anyway) try to latch on to any information you give it. It will notice things in the first round you want to ignore, such as the color of the sake, imperfections like scratches on the glass, the position or angle of the label bearing the number on the underside, and slight differences in the amount of sake in the glass. There is a lot of other distracting information that the mind will try to use to help us. "Ah!" it will say. "That glass with the slightly off-center label was in position two last time!" Or perhaps, "This sake is the darkest of them all. I can look for this in round two." These are perfectly true observations, but you will not be relying on your senses of smell and taste, and the whole purpose of the exercise must be to isolate the flavors and aromas.

The less you know the better. If possible, have someone else pour the sake in the first round for you. Try to put in enough at first to last you two rounds. (Limiting the amount of sake you are allowed to taste is yet another way to sharpen your senses.) Or if you pour yourself, gather the glasses randomly in one spot, then quickly pour a sake into each, then later look at the bottom and place them in their numerical positions. Ignorance is power; not knowing which sake is where is best.

Between rounds, try to be sure the amount of sake left in each glass is the same, lest you use that information against yourself later. Have someone else mix them, or just do it long enough to thoroughly confuse yourself.

As you improve, give yourself a time limit of one or two minutes to taste each sake. One will rarely have much time when tasting in the real world.

* * *

There are certainly other ways to improve your sake-tasting skills. Fortunately, your experience in tasting other things—including but not limited to wine—is transferable. If you have such experience, you may be farther along than you think.

As mentioned in the chapter on regionality, tasting sake will not be exactly like tasting wine, where you learn to nail the age, the region, and the grape variety. But the practices outlined here will make sake even more enjoyable, help you to assess quality, and perhaps even thrust you into the limelight of local sake cognoscenti, should that appeal to you.

EXPANDING YOUR KNOWLEDGE

In this book you have already gone "beyond the basics." But there is still much to learn about sake. Where and how do you get started?

In almost any big city in the world are beverage shops and restaurants that enthusiastically promote sake and sake culture. Seek them out. Many will have hands-on (palates-on?) courses and events that allow you to do what is really most important: to taste as wide a range of sake as you can. There are capable lecturers and teachers all over these days. Attending these events and meeting these people are a great way to learn.

Four sake-centric retailers in the United States I can recommend are True Sake in San Francisco, Sakaya in New York, Saké Nomi in Seattle, and The Sake Shop in Honolulu. There are more, too, and even more wine shops with dedicated sake souls in residence. Online sake retailers are increasing too, with their accompanying websites providing a rich source of educational material.

My own website (www.sake-world.com), my newsletters, and my other media projects will continue to provide fresh and relevant information about sake; please keep connected! I will for the foreseeable future continue my series of seminars, both simple presentations and the extremely comprehensive Sake Professional Course, a three-to-five-day intensive course on all things sake that is not for the faint of heart. You can learn more about this at my website.

My courses are only one source of proper sake education; there are other sake educators all over whose programs are very worthwhile and valuable. I hesitate to list them as it is hard to know who or what will be around in the future. The internet, as well as the usual suspects on social media, will certainly help you find out who is doing what, where, and when.

The important thing, of course, is to stick with sake. Overall, there is much to be learned, but to sake's credit, you need very little to enjoy it. By far the most important thing you can do is keep close to sake and continue tasting.

Finally, I wholeheartedly recommend visiting Japan. Visiting sake breweries in Japan opens perhaps the most inspiring door to the sake world. The sake industry in Japan is not quite as accessible as the wine world is in terms of visits and walk-in tours, but things are quickly getting better. The Japanese government itself is supporting the initiative, so greater access to sakes tours and events is only a matter of time. But even now, with a little language support, the sake world in Japan is available to you to learn from and explore.

CONCLUSION

In conclusion, there is no conclusion to learning about sake. There is so much more! The sake
world is so rich, diverse, and deep that any single line in any single chapter could be expanded
upon. It is simply not feasible to cover everything in one book. Every rice variety or yeast
strain, each region and *toji* guild, and the more-
art-than-science discipline of pairing sake and
food—all of these warrant much more attention than the fleeting glimpse I have provided
here.

At the beginning of my intensive several-
day sake course, I start off with a page of three
guidelines for understanding sake. I state that
these rules will help people, given time, to
truly come to understand sake. I also suggest
that this page may be the most important one
in the textbook.

These three guidelines are:

1. Everything in the sake world is vague;
   there are very rarely clear answers to any
   question.
2. There are exceptions to just about every
   rule and way of doing things in the sake
   world.
3. Almost anything I say here will sooner or
   later be contradicted by a reliable source.

These three principles can make sake
a frustrating topic for anyone trying to learn
about it. However, they are also what make
sake beautiful, endlessly fascinating, and truly
a never-ending pursuit. Bear them in mind as

you continue, for they will undoubtedly serve you well.

Much is happening in the world of sake as in the world at large. Currently, a changing of the guard is almost complete, from a generation in which sake pretty much sold itself to one that calls for marketing, innovation, and effort. Sake will be promoted and sold differently from here on out. International trade practices are on the cusp of major change, too, as the world continues to shrink; most of these changes *should* be positive for the world of sake.

As importers and distributors in other countries all over the world get serious about sake and start to embrace it as a viable product in their markets, demand and availability should both increase. Most big cities have a thriving sake culture now; it will be enjoyable to watch this trend continue and grow.

But it is vital that the industry in Japan reap the benefits of sake's growth as well. Profitability must improve at all levels, and for that, sake's image needs to improve. Sake needs to become more fashionable if not downright sexy and cool. The industry needs to make sake more approachable and more easily understood. As much as it seems that many people around the world have come to know and understand sake, there are disturbingly many who are still clueless.

Undoubtedly, the brewers and distributors are well aware of these challenges. The Japanese government itself is putting more effort into worldwide sake promotion, as well as developing more sake-friendly domestic practices and principles.

But there is still much to be done. I think one key point is ensuring that the culture behind sake is conveyed along with the beverage. It can and should be said that sake embodies the culture of Japan itself. The depth of meaning, the attention to the tiniest details, the relentless pursuit of the pinnacles of the brewing craft—a

kikizake-noryoku: one's sake-tasting ability

kimoto: traditional method of brewing that fosters the production of lactic acid to aid the proliferation of yeast; it is like *yamahai-shikomi* but requires tedious pole-mixing by hand

koji, koji-kin: *Aspergillus oryzae,* a mold sprinkled on rice that helps convert the rice's starch into the sugar the yeast uses in fermentation

koshu: "old" sake, which may mean sake aged by intention or by mistake

kura: sake brewery, short for *sakagura*

kurabito: "people of the *kura*," that is, the sake brewery workers

kuramoto: family that owns the sake brewery

masu: drinking vessel made of cryptomeria wood; traditionally a rice-measuring scoop

Miyamizu: "Shrine Water"; hard water prized by sake brewers in the Nada region

moromi: fermenting mash in the sake brewing process

moto: yeast starter

muroka: sake that has not been charcoal filtered

nama, namazake: sake that has not been pasteurized

nigori, nigorizake: cloudy sake made by allowing some of the rice lees through into the final product

nihonshu-do: Sake Meter Value, or SMV, used to denote the density of sake relative to water; popularly but unreliably used to predict dryer (higher value) and sweeter (lower value) sake

nurukan: sake drunk tepid or lukewarm

o-choko: traditional small sake drinking cup, usually made of decorated pottery

okegai/oke-uri: the practice of buying/selling sake between breweries to supplement production

sakagura: sake brewery, often shortened to *kura*

seimai-buai: percentage indicating the amount of rice grain remaining after milling

-shu: suffix meaning "alcoholic" beverage, often dropped (i.e., *ginjo* is the same as *ginjo-shu*)

shuzo kotekimai: rice especially designated for sake making *sokujo-moto*: a modern, speedier form of sake brewing developed to replace *kimoto* and *yama-hai* methods.

toji: master brewer

tokkuri: decorated ceramic vessel traditionally used to pour sake into drinking cups or glasses

tokubetsu: "special" sake that may meet certain criteria for milling or rice quality or may have some other characteristic that the brewer considers worthy of attention

tokutei meishoshu: "special designation sake," the top six premium sake grades of *junmai daiginjo, daiginjo, junmai ginjo, ginjo, junmai,* and *honjozo*

usu-nigori: "thin" nigori with only a small amount of rice dust left after filtering

yamahai-shikomi: traditional method of brewing that fosters the production of lactic acid to aid the proliferation of yeast; it is like **kimoto** but does not require tedious pole-mixing by hand

yanetsuki-kobo: "yeast clinging to the rafters," that is, natural yeast from a brewery's ambient air used for fermentation instead of purchased varieties

Zenkoku Shinshu Kanpyokai: known in English as the Annual Japan Sake Awards, a national tasting competition

INDEX